Pokémon Snap

Jason R. Rich

SYBEX
San Francisco Paris Düsseldorf Soest London

Pokémon Snap

Associate Publisher: **Roger Stewart**

Contracts and Licensing Manager: **Kristine O'Callaghan**

Acquisitions and Publications Manager: **Dan Brodnitz**

Associate Managing Editor Game Books: **Kari Brooks**

Acquisitions and Developmental Editor: **Tory McLearn**

Editor: **Carol Henry**

Production Editor: **Gemma O'Sullivan**

Proofreader: **Andrea Fox**

Book Design and Production: **Van Winkle Design Group**

Cover Designer: **Calyx Design**

Library of Congress Card Number: 99-65191

ISBN: 0-7821-2666-9

Manufactured in the United States of America

10 9 8 7 6 5 4 3 2 1

To everyone at Creatures, Inc.,

Game Freak, Inc., and

Nintendo responsible

for creating the

Pokémon Snap game

and making Pokémon an

incredible phenomenon

throughout the world!

Pokémon Snap

Acknowledgments

As always, my sincere gratitude goes out to my family and to my two closest and dearest friends, Mark Giordani and Ellen Bromfield, for their never-ending love and support! (Congratulations to Ellen on her engagement to Sandy!)

Also, thanks once again to Roger Stewart, Dan Brodnitz, and Jordan Gold at Sybex for approving the Pathways to Adventure concept and allowing me to work on this third book in the series. I'd also like to thank Tory McLearn, Carol Henry, Diana Van Winkle, Gemma O'Sullivan, Andrea Fox, Kari Brooks, Señoria Bilbo-Brown, and Judy Jigarjian for their hard work on this project.

Without the ongoing support from Susan Eisner and Susan Simpson at Leisure Concepts, as well as the folks in Nintendo of America's licensing department—including Juana Tingdale, Ellen Enrico, Cammy Budd, and Jennifer Loftus—this book would not have been possible. A very special thank-you also goes out to Michael Leslie at Nintendo, who showed me many of the secrets behind the Pokémon Snap video game.

I'd also like to thank Howard Lincoln, Peter Main, George Harrison, Perrin Kaplan, Beth Llewelyn, Scott Pelland, and Gail Tilden from Nintendo of America, as well as Eileen Tanner, Reilly Brennan, and the rest of the Golin/Harris gang, for their ongoing support.

Finally, thanks to you, the reader. It is my greatest wish that you find reading Pokémon Snap—Pathways to Adventure as exciting as playing the Nintendo 64 game itself.

To learn more about my other books, or to let me know what you think about this one, please visit my Web site at http://www.jasonrich.com. I look forward to receiving your e-mails!

—Jason R. Rich

Pokémon Snap

Pokémon Snap

Pokémon Snap

Introduction

Welcome to the World of Pokémon and the Pathways to Adventure book series!

The Pokémon phenomenon started with the original Pokémon video game for the Nintendo Game Boy system. These days, people everywhere are playing Pokémon video games on Game Boy and Nintendo 64. They're also playing the collectible trading card game, watching the animated TV series, reading Pokémon comics, and playing with the ever-growing selection of Pokémon toys.

As you'll soon discover, Pokémon Snap offers a totally new type of Pokémon experience—the video game itself is in full-color and in 3D! In this game, a young photographer named Todd embarks on a quest to help Professor Oak create the PKMN Report, a research project that focuses on the wild Pokémon living on Pokémon Island.

The great thing about games like Pokémon Snap is that there are many ways to play and ultimately beat the game. While this book offers one possible path Todd takes to complete his objectives, when you actually play the game, the choices you make and the actions you take can be different.

Pokémon Snap

Each book in the Pathways to Adventure series tells the exciting story behind a popular video game in a very special way—whatever happens to the main characters in the story also happens in the game! So, by reading any of the Pathways to Adventure books, you'll learn tips and strategies for beating the game that book is based upon (which, in this case, is Pokémon Snap for the Nintendo 64).

Throughout this book, the first time each type of Pokémon is mentioned, a high scoring snap shot appears. The poses of each Pokémon in the photos are based on the shot ultimately added to the PKMN Report. To take a similar photo yourself when playing the game, you may have to wait until later in the adventure.

To learn more about the other books in the Pathways to Adventure series or to let us know what you think about this book, point your Web browser to http://www.sybex.com.

Pokémon Snap

Chapter 1

Todd Meets Professor Oak

The World of Pokémon is a wonderful place where people young and old spend their free time doing a very special thing—they catch and raise wild Pokémon and then enter them into competitions. Virtually everyone wants to someday become the World's Greatest Pokémon Master.

What? You don't know what a Pokémon is?

These remarkable creatures live in the wild; they are small but very powerful and intelligent. Some people catch Pokémon and raise them as pets, but most train them to compete against other Pokémon. There are more than 150 kinds of Pokémon, each with its own look, abilities, and special powers.

Professor Oak is a famous Pokémon expert. Because he's had so much practice training and studying Pokémon, people call him the "Pokémon Prof" and have a lot of respect for him. With the help of a young boy named Ash, the Professor created the Pokédex, a computerized "encyclopedia" containing information about all known Pokémon. An extremely smart and kind man, Professor Oak wants to understand Pokémon even better. Now that he's retired from raising and training Pokémon, he has dedicated his life to studying them and learning as much as he can about them.

As part of his research, Professor Oak helped to establish Pokémon Island, a sanctuary for the many types of wild Pokémon. On this island, in a top-secret location, Pokémon live carefree in their natural habitat. On the island, the creatures can't be captured by Pokémon trainers and are also protected from members of Team Rocket, a society of evil Pokémon trainers.

Everyone knows Professor Oak has more experience with Pokémon than anyone else.

Professor Oak has never allowed anyone to visit Pokémon Island. After guiding Ash to complete the Pokédex, the Professor wanted to continue his teaching and research by studying and taking pictures of wild Pokémon in their natural habitats. His ambitious goal was to create the PKMN Report, which would have colorful photographs and a ton of information about each and every type of wild Pokémon living on the island.

Professor Oak has searched everywhere for the perfect assistant to help him create the PKMN Report. The Professor needed someone who was curious and smart and able to take excellent photographs. Most importantly, the person he selected had to be interested in studying the Pokémon, not capturing and training them.

The bright young person he finally selected for this important task was Todd, a teenager with an outgoing personality and reddish-brown hair. His hobby was taking pictures. In fact, wherever Todd went, he always carried a camera on his shoulder and was ready to snap a photo. Todd was the perfect person for this assignment!

Professor Oak chooses Todd to be his research assistant. Todd will explore Pokémon Island and take pictures of the wild Pokémon living there.

For many months, Professor Oak worked on developing a special contraption called the Zero-One to help his research. When he was finished, he sent Todd a letter, inviting him to Pokémon Island. When Todd arrived at the lab, the Pokémon Prof proudly showed off his invention and gave Todd a demonstration. The Zero-One was an all-terrain vehicle specifically designed to help Todd safely explore every area of Pokémon Island.

The bright-yellow Zero-One was a self-running vehicle jam-packed with special features and secret functions. It was awesome—it could drive along land, float in water, hover in the air, and travel along special tracks. It was waterproof and fireproof, and could withstand both high heat and sub-zero temperatures. This contraption was ready to navigate even the toughest paths on the island.

To help Todd travel safely through each part of Pokémon Island, the Professor has invented a special transport machine called the Zero-One.

Pokémon Island was a mysterious and beautiful place, filled with exotic Pokémon along with many surprises. Professor Oak explained to Todd that each time he set off to explore a section of Pokémon Island, the Zero-One would be set on autopilot. Instead of having to steer the vehicle, the eager young photographer could focus most of his attention on taking pictures.

While riding in this amazing high-tech vehicle, Todd would be able to look in all directions—left, right, up, down, in front of him, or behind him. A good thing, since wild Pokémon could show up at any moment. Once his journey began, the young photographer had to be ready to snap pictures every second of the way.

Todd would be super-safe no matter where he went. The Professor had made the Zero-One smart, so it would automatically adjust itself to whatever part of the island it was in. Todd wouldn't get hurt, and neither would the wild Pokémon living on the island.

After Professor Oak demonstrated all the levers, dials, and gadgets on the Zero-One, he showed Todd a large map of Pokémon Island. It was divided into six clearly marked sections. The Professor told Todd he'd be exploring each area separately. His job was to take photos of all the wild Pokémon living within each section of the island.

According to Professor Oak's map, Pokémon Island is divided into six areas.

Based on the extensive research the Professor had already done, he knew there were 63 types of Pokémon living on Pokémon Island. Since these were wild creatures living in their natural habitats, Todd could expect to find Water-type Pokémon in water-filled areas, for example, and Fire-type Pokémon would be in the warmer climates, such as near the volcano.

To complete the PKMN Report, Todd would need to take the best snapshot possible of each type of Pokémon. The Professor explained that he would evaluate the pictures and award points for each one. Todd would return to the Professor's lab and meet with him after each expedition.

The number of points the young photographer received for each of his snapshots would be based on several things, including the size of the Pokémon in the picture. Close-up shots earned more points, too, and so did a picture showing the Pokémon in a special pose. And if the photo captured a Pokémon doing something out of the ordinary, Professor Oak awarded more bonus points!

Another way for Todd to earn points was to use the skills he'd gained by practicing so much with his camera. For instance, the Professor wanted photos that were in focus, so the Pokémon could be seen clearly. He explained that Todd should try to get the Pokémon looking directly into the camera and perfectly centered in the frame of each picture. Todd knew this wasn't going to be an easy task, especially since the wild Pokémon were free to roam happily around. He doubted they'd just sit still and pose for the camera, at the exact moment he wanted them to!

Todd could earn even more bonus points for taking pictures featuring several of the same-type Pokémon in a single shot.

Luckily, Todd could bring along plenty of film for his trusty camera. Each time he traveled through an area of the island, he'd be able to take a total of 60 shots. From those pictures, he could select the very best ones to show to the Professor. The pictures of each Pokémon type that won a place in the PKMN Report would be the pictures that scored the most points.

Early on, Todd would ride in the Zero-One through each section of the island and take pictures of the Pokémon that were out in the open and visible. As he gained more experience and earned more points, the Professor said he'd give Todd some special tools to help him take the more challenging shots—of Pokémon that were hiding, sleeping, or just being shy. These tools included Pokémon Food, Pester Balls, a Poké Flute, and the Dash Engine upgrade for the Zero-One. When Todd earned these special rewards, the Professor would explain how to use them to take better pictures.

As he listened to the Professor tell him all about Pokémon Island, Todd could see that he would need to return to each section of the island many times. It would be especially important for the young researcher to go back to a section each time he received a new tool from the Professor. Every item Todd earned would help him uncover new secrets and allow him to photograph all the different types of Pokémon.

Todd loves to take pictures. He always carries his trusty camera with him no matter where he goes.

Todd couldn't believe how lucky he was to be selected by the famous Pokémon Prof for this very important research project. Helping the Professor complete the PKMN Report was a tremendous responsibility and a huge honor. It was truly a dream come true for Todd! The young photographer could hardy wait to hop into the Zero-One and begin exploring the island in this awesome vehicle.

Even though Todd was very excited, he was also a bit scared. After all, he knew that some parts of the island could be dangerous. Nobody really knew how the untamed Pokémon were going to react to his presence.

Even though Todd was very excited, he was also a bit scared. After all, he knew that some parts of the island could be dangerous. Nobody really knew how the untamed Pokémon were going to react to his presence. Professor Oak reminded Todd that the Zero-One would keep him safe at all times. This gave the young photographer courage as he prepared to embark on his incredible adventure.

To get ready, Todd put on his favorite outfit—a striped shirt, a pair of shorts, and his most comfortable hiking shoes. He also loaded his camera with a fresh roll of film.

Once Todd was ready to leave, Professor Oak explained that "the Zero-One vehicle constantly moves toward the Goal Gate." These special Goal Gates were at the end of each area of the island. The gates were large yellow archways that would transport the Zero-One back to the lab as each of Todd's excursions came to an end.

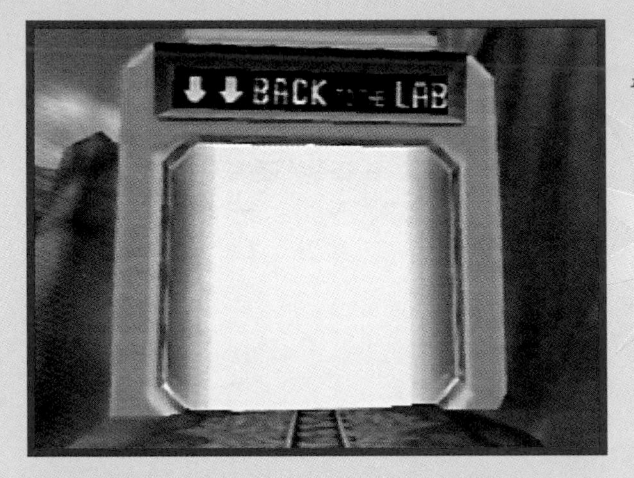

At the end of each path on Pokémon Island is a magical Goal Gate that brings Todd and the Zero-One back to the Professor's lab.

"I'm counting on you, Todd," said the Professor as he waved good-bye and sent his young researcher toward the first area of Pokémon Island: the Beach. The engines of the Zero-One revved up and Todd took off.

His adventure was about to begin!

Pokémon
Snap
Chapter 2
Todd Visits
the Beach
01
SNAP

Pokémon Snap

It was a bright, sunny afternoon on Pokémon Island, and Todd could hardly wait—he was thrilled to be starting his exciting quest to photograph the wild Pokémon in their natural environments.

Todd arrives for the very first time on Pokémon Island and heads for the Beach.

After leaving Professor Oak's lab, Todd arrived at the edge of Pokémon Island riding in the bright-yellow Zero-One. Here he was, near the coast of the island at the beginning of what looked like a railroad track snaking along a beautiful sandy beach.

Todd's camera was loaded with film and his zoom lens was powered up. As he felt the cool ocean breeze blow through his hair, Todd knew he was ready to begin his adventure.

To photograph all of the different types of wild Pokémon, Todd needed to search everywhere and work quickly. Once he began exploring, the Zero-One vehicle would automatically keep moving forward—toward the Goal Gates that marked the end of each area of the island. Luckily, the Professor had added a special sensing device to the Zero-One that made it automatically slow down to avoid crashing into Pokémon in its path. This high-tech, all-terrain vehicle would be on autopilot most of the time, allowing Todd to focus his attention on taking pictures.

Within seconds of landing on the Beach, Todd noticed three Pidgey soaring overhead. He grabbed his camera and started shooting pictures. To take the best pictures possible, he waited for the birdlike Pokémon to fly forward, right into the center of the camera's viewfinder. Todd quickly discovered that perfect timing was the key to getting the best pictures. He knew that capturing several of the same type of Pokémon in one shot would make a more impressive photo.

PIDGEY™
Number: 16
Course: Beach
Photo Score: 4,830

Just as the Pidgey flew off into the distance, a large Doduo, with its two heads and bright-yellow beaks, ran across the track. Snap! Todd managed to capture the Doduo on film, just in the nick of time!

DODUO™
Number: 84
Course: Beach
Photo Score: 2,900

Suddenly, off in the distance, Todd heard a funny sound. "Pika-Pika-Pi-ka-chu"—and then he couldn't believe his eyes and ears. Only minutes after arriving on Pokémon Island, the young photographer saw his first Pikachu! It was playing on the sandy beach, just a few feet away from a surfboard. What a funny sight it would be to see a Pikachu surfing, Todd thought. He wondered what it would take to lure the Pikachu to the surfboard.

PIKACHU™
Number: 25
Course: Beach
Photo Score: 6,240

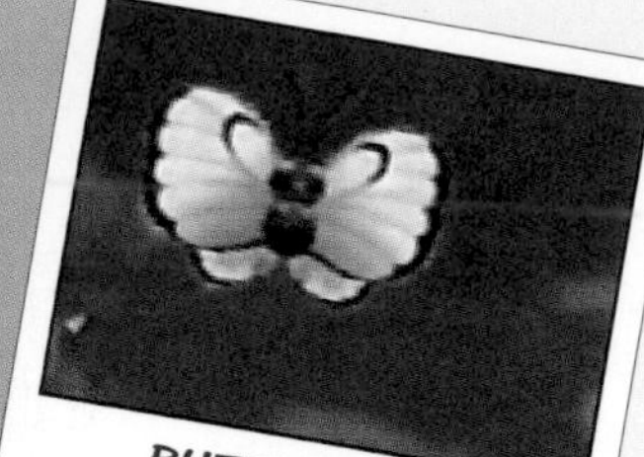

BUTTERFREE™
Number: 12
Course: Beach
Photo Score: 3,760

The Zero-One sped onwards, giving Todd only a little time to watch the Pikachu play. Then, floating over a flowerbed on the right side of the track was a beautiful blue Butterfree. Click! Click! Todd snapped some photos of the butterfly-like creature, zooming in as close as possible and, as always, getting the lovely Pokémon in the center of the frame.

Looking beyond the Butterfree, just past the nearby palm tree, Todd noticed a Pokémon with a great head atop a long neck swimming in the ocean. It reminded him of a mythical sea creature! It was a ways off in the distance, so Todd used his zoom lens to focus in close. This Pokémon was a blue Lapras, and it stayed in sight only for a few seconds before diving back underwater—but not before Todd's quick reaction. He clicked the camera's shutter just in time!

LAPRAS™
Number: 131
Course: Beach
Photo Score: 2,940

Back on land, the young researcher noticed an enormous sleeping Pokémon below two flying Butterfree. Because it wouldn't wake up and face the camera, Todd couldn't identify this Pokémon. He'd have to come back to the Beach again, after figuring out a way to get the lazy creature's attention.

MEOWTH™
Number: 52
Course: Beach
Photo Score: 3,660

Looking up to his right, Todd noticed a cute but shy Meowth peeking its head over a cliff. Click! Click! Got it! He'd had only a second to catch it on film, but Todd was fast when it came to using his camera. This shot of the Meowth looking directly into the camera would earn extra points.

The dependable Zero-One kept moving steadily forward. Todd saw more Meowth, Pidgey, and Butterfree. To his left, in a group of bushes, leaves rustled in the breeze. Something was hiding in the bushes, but Todd couldn't tell what it was.

Was Todd imagining it, or was the Lapras actually smiling?

Todd swung his head to the right and spotted the Lapras creature again. It had come closer to the beach. Was Todd imagining it, or was the Lapras actually smiling? Excellent! With a click of the camera's shutter, Todd caught the beautiful, friendly creature on film. This was a much better shot than the first one.

EEVEE™
Number: 133
Course: Beach
Photo Score: 2,660

Farther on, Todd snapped a stunning photo of a baby Eevee running in between a group of rocks on the left side of the track. The Eevee was chasing another wild Pokémon that the curious photographer couldn't immediately identify. It was round and much larger than the Eevee. The two Pokémon appeared to be friends. This would be a great shot, Todd knew, because it showed two different Pokémon types getting along with each other and having fun.

Zipping along, the Zero-One moved smoothly down the track, showing Todd more of the Beach area. The eager photographer looked out to sea to his right and noticed two Lapras swimming very close to the land. This was Todd's best opportunity yet to snap these graceful sea Pokémon, and he knew when he pressed the shutter that it was a shot worth bonus points.

It's a game of Pokémon chase—two Pokémon playing in the wild.

Two Lapras swim near the shoreline, allowing Todd to photograph them close up.

Moments later, he saw a Kangaskhan with its back turned. Even though the young photographer couldn't get the big mean-looking creature to look at him, he took a picture anyway. Yes, he'd have to return later for a better shot. But the PKMN Report could always be updated with better and higher-scoring photos of the Pokémon.

KANGASKHAN™
Number:115
Course: Beach
Photo Score: 3,960

Looking directly ahead, Todd noticed he was approaching the Goal Gate. He rode in closer, and a brilliant

white light shone out from under the gleaming archway. Wondrously, Todd was transported back to Professor Oak's lab!

In one miraculous moment, Todd is transported through the Goal Gate's bright white light back to the Professor's lab.

On this first trip to the Beach, Todd used 33 of the 60 pictures on the roll of film in his camera. He would be given a new roll of film at the start of each expedition. Now that he had returned to the lab, it was time to choose which photos he'd show to the professor and eventually include in the PKMN Report. Todd examined each photo, selecting the ones that showed at least one Pokémon centered in the frame and looking directly into the camera. He looked for close-ups especially—the Professor would want those, for sure, in the report.

PIDGEY™
Number: 16
Type: Normal/Flying

When Todd showed Professor Oak the first set of pictures, his mentor studied each of them carefully. He awarded points for each photo based on the size of the Pokémon, its pose, and Todd's photographic technique. By snapping a

Pokémon doing something special, like a Pidgey using its Gust technique, Todd earned bonus points, which made him very happy.

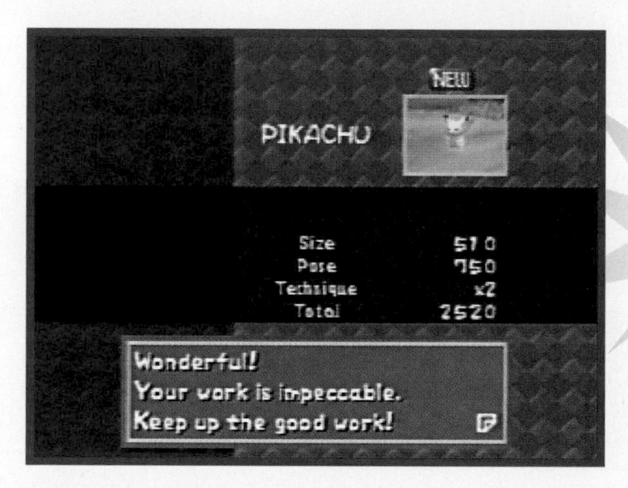

Professor Oak is delighted with Todd's first set of snapshots.

"The Pokémon is right in the middle of the frame. Wonderful!" said the Professor. "Your work is impeccable." Getting this kind of praise from the Pokémon Prof was a great reward for Todd, who was trying his hardest to impress his teacher.

Then it was time for the proud photographer to return to the Beach and take another round of snapshots, trying for some Pokémon he'd missed during his first trek into the area. As it turned out, it was well worth the trip. Not only did he get some really super shots, but he soon discovered that his photo-taking abilities had improved. Todd was now earning at least 2,000 points each for many of his new photos. At this point he had added pictures of over seven types of Pokémon to the PKMN Report. "Welcome back!" said the Professor. "You are doing a fine job, Todd."

BUTTERFREE™
Number: 12
Type: Bug/Flying

MAGIKARP™
Number: 129
Type: Water

Of course, there were still many more photos to take in the Beach area. Todd needed shots of a Butterfree, Pidgey, Meowth, Doduo, Chansey, Kangaskhan, Scyther, Lapras, Eevee, and a Snorlax—snapshots worth at least 2,000 to 5,000 points each. The Professor had told Todd he'd be seeing many Pikachu and fishlike Magikarp throughout the island, so snapping pictures of these Pokémon wasn't a top priority.

The Professor had told Todd he'd be seeing many Pikachu and fishlike Magikarp throughout the island.

Todd decided the best strategy to take during his first few trips to various parts of the island was to snap photos of as many Pokémon as possible, even if the shots weren't perfect. He could come back later and get higher-scoring pictures once he had the special tools Professor Oak had promised. But, the young photographer had to first prove his abilities by earning those high total point scores.

PIKACHU™
Number: 25
Type: Electric

For now, getting all of the necessary photos in the Beach area for the PKMN Report would have to wait a bit. Professor Oak was so satisfied with the experience Todd had gained, he knew his young assistant was ready to begin exploring the next section of the island: the Tunnel. This new area was inhabited by many more types of Pokémon to study and photograph.

As the two looked at the map of Pokémon Island, Professor Oak gave his helper directions to the Tunnel, and permission to explore it. It was time to see what other exciting photo opportunities were waiting!

Chapter 3
Tunnel of Surprises

Todd's visit to Pokémon Island's Beach had given him a taste of what being a Pokémon researcher is all about. He was enthusiastic and ready for more. As the Zero-One carried him deeper toward the heart of the island—this time, to the mysterious Tunnel—Todd knew there was adventure in store!

With the help of Professor Oak, Todd plots a course toward the dark and mysterious Tunnel.

Here, he'd no doubt see firsthand many of the fascinating Pokémon he'd only read about in the Pokédex. Ash, the boy who had recently worked with the Professor to complete the Pokédex, was now a famous Pokémon Master.

Todd had learned from the Professor that there was an abandoned Power Plant located in the Tunnel. He couldn't wait to check it out because he suspected it was something special. When his transport came to a stop near the entrance of the Tunnel, the young photographer noticed that this time there was no railroad-like track. Instead, there was a narrow path. It was just wide enough for the Zero-One vehicle to follow.

After setting the controls to make the Zero-One start traveling forward, Todd eagerly grabbed his camera and positioned himself to begin snapping pictures.

ELECTRODE™
Number: 101
Course: Tunnel
Photo Score: 4,400

Looking to the right, near the entrance of the Tunnel, he spotted another Pikachu. It was standing close to a strange object with a red light on it. Though he already had several excellent pictures of a Pikachu, it couldn't hurt to take more. Click! Click! went the camera.

Just then, a large round Electrode came rolling over from the left, and several more appeared as the Zero-One passed through the Tunnel's entrance. Click! Click!

ELECTABUZZ™
Number: 125
Course: Tunnel
Photo Score: 2,910

A yellow Electabuzz was just ahead, waving its arms as Todd's vehicle approached. The Electabuzz seemed to be guarding the Tunnel's entrance. Unfortunately, the creature stubbornly refused to look directly into Todd's camera. Snap! Todd took a picture anyway.

Looking up, Todd noticed several Kakuna hanging from the ceiling of the Tunnel. He was amazed at how many different types of Pokémon lived in this cold, unlit place—he'd come across four already! To make sure he captured all of them on film, Todd kept turning from left to right, and even occasionally looked behind him. He discovered that by turning quickly around in a complete circle, he could make the Zero-One slow down a bit, giving him extra time to snap pictures. The vehicle also slowed down when Todd was looking backwards. These were handy tricks to keep in mind for treks around the island.

KAKUNA™
Number: 14
Course: Tunnel
Photo Score: 4,260

ZUBAT™
Number: 41
Course: Tunnel
Photo Score: 1,480

The Zero-One carried Todd forward steadily, and he could see that he was approaching a pair of huge metal doors. What was behind them? Professor Oak's curious young assistant was about to find out. Though the doors appeared to be locked, they magically opened as the Zero-One drew near. Suddenly, out soared a bat-like Zubat, flying directly at Todd. He only had a few short seconds to snap a picture before the dark-colored creature was gone. He wondered how that quick shot would turn out...

Then, off to his right, there it was–
the broken Power Plant.

Then, off to his right, there it was—the broken Power Plant. It was a very odd looking metal gizmo that clearly hadn't been used in a long time—at least, not since Pokémon Island had become a Pokémon sanctuary. On the left, across the path from the Power Plant, was another adorable Pikachu. Playing near a large and colorful egg, it kept laughing and saying "Pi-ka-chu!" Hmmm, maybe there was something inside the egg...

Just ahead Todd saw another set of the big metal doors. Before passing through these doors, which again suddenly opened, Todd spotted a dark, flying, ball-shaped creature to his left. He couldn't identify it, but he took pictures anyway. He figured the Professor would know what type of Pokémon this was.

As the steely doors swung open once again, another Zubat came flying toward the Zero-One, this time giving Todd an excellent photo opportunity. Whoosh! The Zubat

was approaching so fast and came so close, Todd almost had to duck to avoid it. Luckily it veered away from the vehicle at the last second.

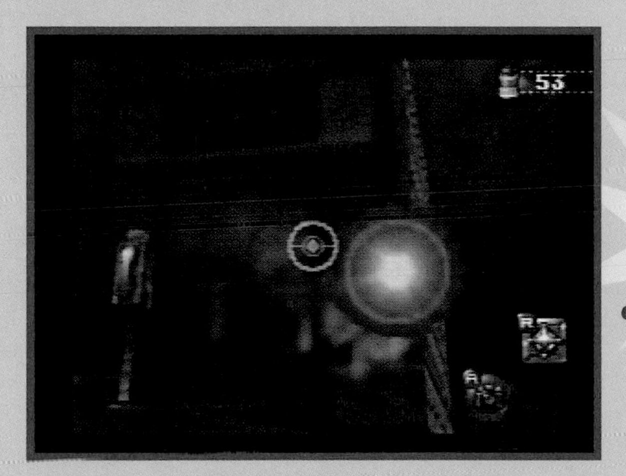

Even by looking directly at this round Flying-type Pokémon, Todd couldn't figure out what it was.

Next, the young photographer spotted two Electabuzz Pokémon off to the right, facing a small building. Though they were turned away from him, Todd could see they were smashing their fists against the wall. They didn't appear to be at all happy. To the left of his vehicle, Todd noticed another of the mysterious Flying-type Pokémon that he couldn't identify. His camera's shutter clicked away as he captured all of these intriguing sights on film.

DIGLETT™
Number: 50
Course: Tunnel
Photo Score: 3,420

There on the left was another Pikachu—and this time it was playing with a Diglett. The Diglett had popped its small brown head up from the ground. Click! Click! Todd happily snapped a high-points picture that included both Pokémon.

MAGNEMITE™
Number: 81
Type: Electric

Meanwhile, the trusty Zero-One was moving on through the Tunnel. Looking ahead, Todd saw the Goal Gate, with several Magnemite in front of it. But these Pokémon wouldn't allow themselves to be photographed.

As he neared the Goal Gate, Todd noticed another cavelike area to his right, blocked by some hefty rocks. An Electrode, with a very serious look on its face, stood guard. What was in that cave? wondered the Professor's assistant...

Todd had come across many mysterious objects in the Tunnel. Clearly, he would need to return so he could find out what they were. He also wanted another chance to photograph the many types of Pokémon he'd missed on this first trip here.

Then the Zero-One passed through the Goal Gate, and the brilliant light enveloped the young photographer and transported him back to the lab.

As soon as Todd developed his pictures, he discovered something surprising. On film, he was able to see that the mysterious, dark Flying-type Pokémon were actually Haunter. For some strange, unexplained reason, they were easy to recognize in the photos, even though in person their identity was hidden. Luckily, he had taken several excellent pictures of these creatures and was now able to choose the perfect shot to present to Professor Oak.

HAUNTER™
Number: 93
Course: Tunnel
Photo Score: 4,000

The Pokémon Prof was pleased with most of the photos Todd had taken in the Tunnel area. But when he saw the shot of the Electabuzz, he said, "It's not very good. You were close, but you see...It disappoints Pokémon to be photographed from behind."

The Professor also suggested that Todd take a better shot of the Kakuna. "You were close. But It would have been better if it were a larger shot," explained Todd's teacher.

KAKUNA™
Number: 14
Type: Bug/Poison

Todd now knew what his goal was for the next trip through the Tunnel: better pictures of an Electabuzz and a Kakuna were needed for the PKMN Report. But, there was something else in store for Todd, as well. By the time all of his photos were examined by the Professor, he had earned a total of 23,150 points and had captured 13 different kinds of Pokémon on film! "If you get 850 more points on your PKMN Report, you'll get something cool," promised Todd's mentor. So Todd returned to the Tunnel to gather more photos, anxious to find out what the "something cool" would be.

The second trip through the Tunnel passed quickly, and the determined young researcher was able to improve the Diglett's picture. He also caught some other types of Pokémon on film. This earned him the extra points he needed in order to receive the special reward from the Professor. Afterward, Todd rejoined his teacher and showed off his new snapshots.

"Welcome back!" said Professor Oak when Todd returned to the lab. "You take pictures at a good pace. To make your work easier, here is a present for you. It will come in handy for taking Pokémon pictures. Would you like to be closer with Pokémon? Then use this apple-shaped Pokémon Food."

Professor Oak gives Todd a supply of Pokémon Food as his reward for earning over 24,000 points.

Wow, Pokémon Food! Todd could use the food to lure wild Pokémon closer to his vehicle and get better-than-ever pictures.

Wow, Pokémon Food! Todd could use the food to lure wild Pokémon closer to his vehicle and get better-than-ever pictures. "Pokémon in the distance will happily come closer when you use this item," said the Pokémon Prof. He also pointed out that Todd would be able to throw the food a greater distance if he aimed slightly upward when he tossed it toward a Pokémon.

Now that Todd had food for the Pokémon, he again returned to the Tunnel. This time, he tossed the food at all of the Pokémon he encountered. It worked! Pokémon, including the Kakuna and Electabuzz, came closer to Todd and faced his camera. These photos would be awesome!

ELECTABUZZ™
Number: 125
Type: Electric

On his next trip through the Tunnel, Todd tossed food directly at the big, round Electrode guarding the blocked cave. Boom! The Electrode caused an explosion and the rocks blocking the entrance crumbled. Todd could see that it wasn't just a cave— it was a secret entrance to the Volcano area of Pokémon Island!

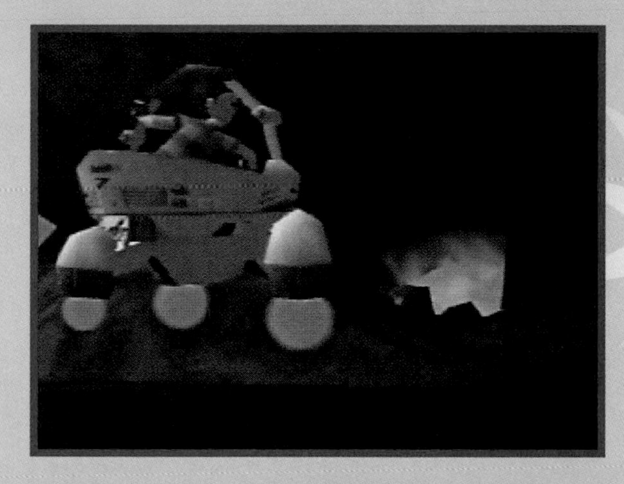

As soon as Todd tosses food directly at the Electrode guarding the blocked cave, the Electric-type Pokémon creates an explosion that reveals a secret passageway.

Excited and wondering about the mouth of the blocked cave, Todd returned to the lab. Professor Oak greeted him and explained, "Todd, you found a split in the path! According to my research, that split should link to a new course. You should go right away!" So, checking out his Pokémon Island map, Todd plotted a course to the Volcano area of the island, where his adventure would continue.

Many times during his journey through Pokémon Island, Professor Oak's assistant had to be very clever in order to snap some of the pictures he so desperately needed for the PKMN Report. He was smart and determined. Professor Oak would not regret choosing Todd for this assignment.

Pokémon Snap

Chapter 4

Todd Explores the Volcano

Things were about to heat up! Todd had discovered the course to the Volcano area at the end of the Tunnel, and the Professor had urged him to resume his trek. The Zero-One passed through the secret passageway, carrying Todd into this place of fire and heat and strange smells. All around him, the young Pokémon researcher could see pools of bubbling hot lava. The heat was intense! He could smell the volcanic ash clouding the air.

Having studied the Pokédex before his journey began, Todd knew that he'd find Fire-type Pokémon in this environment. He had plenty of Pokémon Food with him, and planned to put it to good use. He also felt a little anxious, hoping the Zero-One's special heat-shielding feature would protect him from the open flames he could see shooting into the sky.

Everywhere Todd looks in the Volcano section, there are boiling hot lava pools and giant craters!

Seconds after the Zero-One vehicle reached the entrance of the Volcano area, Todd spotted several horse-like Rapidash galloping freely around the open terrain. Awesome! They appeared to be one with the fire that surrounded them! Raising his trusty camera up to his eye, Todd immediately began snapping pictures as his vehicle moved along.

RAPIDASH™
Number: 78
Course: Volcano
Photo Score: 4,770

As the Zero-One rode past the Rapidash creatures, over to the left was a single Vulpix playing by itself. Todd gladly tossed some Pokémon Food to this cute red Pokémon and took its picture. Looking to the right, he saw two more Vulpix playing together. What an adorable sight—and what a nice photo score he would get by capturing this scene! As the camera's shutter clicked, Todd thought about how this picture would add to the PKMN Report.

VULPIX™
Number: 37
Course: Volcano
Photo Score: 4,550

MAGMAR™
Number: 126
Course: Volcano
Photo Score: 6,140

Turning his attention ahead, the Professor's assistant could see off in the distance a red and yellow, fire-breathing Magmar walking around minding its own business. To get its attention, Todd tossed over some Pokémon Food and then took its picture. A young and hungry Charmander came running over when it saw the food. Click! Click!

Looking forward once again, Todd noticed a big yellow and red egg directly in the Zero-One's path. Oh, no! The vehicle was on a crash course! Thinking fast, he began tossing food at the egg, hoping to knock it out of the way before it got crushed. The food hit the egg. It began to roll. Splash! It fell right into a nearby lava pit.

CHARMANDER™
Number: 4
Course: Volcano
Photo Score: 4,410

Moments later, something wonderful happened. An immense, brightly-colored Moltres spread its flaming wings and emerged from the lava! Astonished, Todd had just a few

MOLTRES™
Number: 146
Course: Volcano
Photo Score: 3,580

quick seconds to capture this lovely flying creature on film. He hurried to press his camera's shutter in time.

As the Moltres flew out of sight, Todd saw two more Magmar playing on a nearby ledge, to the right of the Zero-One. They were practicing their fire-breathing technique. Click! Click! The Professor's assistant happily snapped pictures of the twin fire-breathers. Swinging his head to the left, Todd spotted two more Charmander and caught them on film.

Two twin Magmar practice their fire breathing as Todd passes by.

The Zero-One zipped along, following a narrow path made of hardened lava. As he rode past a small pool of water, Todd thought he might catch a glimpse of a Magikarp or another Water-type Pokémon. He tossed some food into the water. He was in luck! A Magikarp flipped up out of the little pool and then came diving down. It stayed in sight for only a second or two, and Todd had to snap his pictures quickly. He knew he would have better opportunities to get snapshots of Water-type Pokémon later, in other parts of the island. But there was no harm in photographing all the Pokémon he could while visiting the Volcano area.

Looking ahead, the young photographer saw he was rapidly approaching the Goal Gate. Todd took one last glance to each side of the Zero-One, and then behind him, before his vehicle was surrounded by the powerful white light that transported him back to Professor Oak's lab.

Once again, Todd carefully flipped through all the pictures from the Volcano trek and selected only the best ones to show to the Professor. "Oh, what a wonderful pose!" said Professor Oak when he saw his assistant's photo of the Moltres. For this shot, Todd earned an impressive 3,580 points. This really increased his overall PKMN Report point total, which was now at 45,150.

NEW
MOLTRES
Size 440
Pose 1350
Technique x2
Total 3580
Wonderful!
Your work is impeccable.
Keep up the good work!

The Professor gives Todd a very impressive score for his photo of the Moltres.

The Professor's enthusiastic assistant had already taken photos of 19 different kinds of Pokémon for the PKMN Report. "You'll find out what the next course is if you take 3 more Pokémon pictures," said Professor Oak, as he once more congratulated Todd on a job well done.

MOLTRES™
Number: 146
Type: Fire/Flying

Returning to his trusty transport, young Todd set the Zero-One on a course back to the Volcano area. He had reviewed the PKMN Report to check out his point total, and he knew which low-scoring pictures needed to be retaken. As always, he hoped to take more shots and better shots, so he could boost his point score even more.

CHARMELEON™
Number: 5
Course: Volcano
Photo Score: 2,560

This time, when he traveled through the Volcano area, Todd managed to snap a photo of a Charmeleon. The Pokémon was standing pretty far away, but as Todd clicked the shutter he knew he could eventually go back and get a better picture later. The rest of his journey passed quickly.

For his next trip to the island after visiting Professor Oak, the young photographer decided he should backtrack a bit and revisit some of the areas he had already seen. Now that he had Pokémon Food at his disposal, Todd would be able to use it to tempt several of the Pokémon he'd missed back in the Beach and Tunnel areas.

Returning first to the Beach, Todd remembered his thoughts from the first trip to the Beach. Could he get the Pikachu to approach the surfboard? He figured he'd try tossing several pieces of food between the Pokémon and the surfboard, hoping the creature would be hungry and follow the trail of food. His plan worked! In fact, it worked so well that Todd managed to snap some great shots of Surfing Pikachu! The Professor would be really stoked to see a picture of a Pikachu surfing, and Todd was sure it would earn extra points.

With the help of some tempting Pokémon Food, Todd gets the Pikachu to climb on the surfboard. He snaps several photographs of Surfing Pikachu from different angles.

The Zero-One kept retracing its route through the now familiar Beach area. Looking up, toward the right side of the track, Todd spotted the shy Meowth peeking its head over a cliff. When he tossed it some food, this delightful little Pokémon ran in for the snack. Todd, of course, took its picture. He couldn't believe his luck—first a surfing Pikachu, and now a Meowth!

Looking up, toward the right side of the track, Todd spotted the shy Meowth peeking its head over a cliff. When he tossed it some food, this delightful little Pokémon became so happy, it began to dance!

As the Zero-One again approached the Beach's Goal Gate, Todd tried tossing Pokémon Food at a nearby Kangaskhan. It turned around and walked directly toward the Zero-One. Opening its mouth really wide, it let out a mighty "R-r-r-o-o-a-a-r!" Todd was ready, snapping a photo just before he rode on toward the light of the Goal Gate.

MEOWTH™
Number: 52
Type: Normal

Professor Oak realized Todd had managed to capture over 22 different types of Pokémon on film. He called out to his assistant. "Wait, Todd...Let's return to the lab!" he exclaimed.

Back in the lab, the Professor took out the Pokémon Island map and gave Todd directions to the River section of the island. It was time to give the Zero-One a chance to use its water-navigation features. In the River area, Todd would come face-to-face with several species of Water-type Pokémon.

Pokémon Snap

Chapter 5

Riding the Waves of the River

As Todd continued his exploration of Pokémon Island, he was more and more surprised by how different each of the environments were. So far, he'd been able to explore a beautiful tropical beach, travel below the island's surface, and ride through a maze of lava pools and craters.

At least 10 different Pokémon lived within each area of the island, and Todd had happily photographed them. The PKMN Report was coming along fine. Professor Oak was very pleased with his assistant's progress. The young photographer couldn't wait to check out the next area of Pokémon Island: the River.

The bottom of the Zero-One had sprouted flotation devices!

The Zero-One landed with a gentle splash into the River area. The professor had designed this very special vehicle so it could travel through all areas of the island. The bottom of the Zero-One had sprouted flotation devices!

When the Zero-One lands in the River area, Todd finds out his vehicle can float.

Todd would enjoy a calm and peaceful ride as the Zero-One floated along the winding river. The weather was warm and clear, so it was a perfect setting for taking pictures of the Water-type Pokémon living in this area.

Looking up and to the right of the Zero-One, Todd immediately noticed a series of low cliffs. There was movement in the nearby bushes! Some Pokémon must be hiding there, he thought to himself. Knowing exactly what to do, Todd began tossing food upward onto the cliff, directly at the spot where he thought the Pokémon might be.

Tossing food toward the cliffs gets one Poliwag to move out of the bushes. Later, Todd will use Pester Balls to make all these Pokémon come out.

This made one small, round, blue Poliwag come all the way out. But the rest weren't showing themselves completely just yet, which made good snapshots difficult to get. For now, Todd did the best he could, taking pictures of the Poliwag from a distance. He'd improve this particular entry to the PKMN Report later.

POLIWAG™
Number: 60
Course: River
Photo Score: 2,780

As the Zero-One bobbed along in the water, it floated near a hollow tree stump on the left bank. A green-colored Bulbasaur was hiding inside. The creature's large shell was barely visible, so Todd tried tossing

BULBASAUR™
Number: 1
Course: River
Photo Score: 3,880

food to get it to appear. The Pokémon refused to show itself, however—but then another Bulbasaur came running toward the tree stump and the food. With a bit more food, Todd coaxed this second Bulbasaur into turning to face the camera. Just when this happened, Todd snapped a bunch of pictures.

Looking ahead and to the left, the Professor's assistant saw a fat pink Slowpoke hanging out near the edge of the river. It was taking a drink. Just past this creature, several Shellder were jumping out of the water. Some were facing Todd's camera, so he took a few pictures.

SLOWPOKE™
Number: 79
Course: River
Photo Score: 3,340

Todd had an idea! Maybe by tossing some food between the Slowpoke and the nearby wooden sign, he could get the big pink creature to turn its head and face the sign. It worked—and at the same time, the Slowpoke stuck its tail into the water. Thinking the Slowpoke's tail was food, one of the Shellder clamped onto it. Todd was delighted. He started laughing as he took a picture of this funny scene. After all, it's not every day you see a Slowpoke walking around with a Shellder stuck to its tail!

SHELLDER™
Number: 90
Course: River
Photo Score: 4,300

There was another surprise in store for Todd. Right before his eyes, the Slowpoke evolved into a Slowbro! Click! Click! went the camera. Another Slowpoke was just ahead. Todd again tried getting the second Slowpoke to stick its tail in the water. And again, this

Pokémon evolved when a Shellder nabbed its tail. Hooray! The young photographer knew these snapshots would make a perfect addition to the PKMN Report.

SLOWBRO™
Number: 80
Course: River
Photo Score: 3,480

Suddenly, from out of nowhere, a Magikarp came splashing out of the water. This happened a lot in the River area, so Todd always had to be ready to catch these fishlike creatures on film, before they dove back underwater.

Professor Oak's researcher now could see more Pokémon of several types to his right, to his left, in the water, and even overhead. Curious, he looked up to find several green Metapod hanging from vines. He snapped pictures of these wormlike creatures as he passed below them.

METAPOD™
Number: 11
Course: River
Photo Score: 3,000

The Zero-One continued to float gently down the river. Todd looked ahead and spotted a plump yellow Pokémon happily swimming around in circles. It was a friendly Psyduck! When Todd threw some food at this comical creature, it dove under and then sprang high into the air, creating splashes in the water. This was the perfect moment to take a picture. Todd clicked the shutter button.

PSYDUCK™
Number: 54
Course: River
Photo Score: 3,840

On the right bank of the river, past the Psyduck, Todd was puzzled to see a flat red switch on the ground. What was it doing there? He tried throwing food at it, but nothing happened. The Zero-One floated along without Todd getting any clues at all about the switch.

Pokémon Snap

What is the red switch for, Todd wonders? How can he activate it?

Just above the switch, inside a stone cliff, was a Normal-type Pokémon. The small creature's beak was the same color as the cliff, and Todd almost didn't see it. The Pokémon and the cliff blended together nearly perfectly. For now, there was nothing Todd could do to get the creature's attention.

PSYDUCK™
Number:54
Type: Water

The Zero-One was now traveling through a wide area of the river. Hoping to spot more swimming Pokémon, the eager young researcher kept throwing food into the water as he enjoyed the beautiful scenery around him. To the left, playing among several hollow tree stumps, Todd saw an adorable yellow Pikachu. As soon as he started taking pictures, the Electric-type Pokémon started running around so fast that a trail of white stars appeared behind it.

Todd could hear it yelling "Pi-ka-chu!" but he couldn't get the fast-moving Pokémon to stand still for a picture. He knew he'd need to time this shot perfectly. Capturing Speed Pikachu on film was worth 800 bonus points, and with some careful maneuvering, the talented photographer got it!

Todd watches the Pokémon run around at lightning fast speed. It's Speed Pikachu!

Just ahead was the Goal Gate. But what was that huge metal gate over to the right? It was locked. Aha! Todd figured the strange red switch he'd passed earlier might be what was needed to unlock this gate, but he still had to figure out how to activate that switch!

Todd has a feeling that if he can open the locked gate, he'll find a secret pathway.

The Zero-One floated toward the Goal Gate, and the familiar white light enveloped them. Within moments, Todd found himself safely back in the lab. His first ride through the River area had come to an end.

During this part of his journey, Todd had snapped many wonderful photos, but he had missed several types of Pokémon that lived in the area. Return trips would definitely be necessary.

After Professor Oak examined and graded Todd's pictures, the PKMN Report was worth 62,310 points. "If you get 10,190 more points on your PKMN Report, you'll get something cool," said the Pokémon Prof to Todd. Another reward!

Todd loved surprises. He could hardly wait to see what he'd be given once he earned the necessary points. He wanted to return immediately to the River area and take more photos, which is exactly what he did.

Todd was back on the river, across from the Slowpoke. Nearby, on the right side of his vehicle, he spotted the top of a Pokémon that he hadn't noticed before. Most of it was hiding underground. Only the creature's red and white, mushroom-shaped head was showing. At the moment, Todd couldn't identify what type of Pokémon it was.

During this second trip through the River area, Todd took a handful of much more interesting snapshots of Poliwag, Bulbasaur, Magikarp, and Metapod. These shots would get higher scores and help him win the additional points he needed to get that promised prize.

BULBASAUR™
Number: 1
Type: Grass/Poison

When Todd returned to the lab, he met up again with Professor Oak. "You take pictures at a good pace," said the

Pokémon Prof after looking over Todd's latest group of photos. "To make your work easier, here is a present for you." Now that Todd had earned over 72,500 points, his reward was a generous supply of red-and-blue Pester Balls. These items had a safe but effective repellent spray in them, which would force hiding Pokémon out into the open.

"It will come in handy for taking Pokémon pictures. If you see a place where you think Pokémon might be hiding, use this Pester Ball," added the Professor, as he explained to Todd how these items worked.

Todd was really curious about what Pester Balls could do, so he tried them out as soon as he landed back in the River area.

Hopping back into the Zero-One, Todd again set a course to the River area. Ultimately, he would also need to travel back to other areas of the island, this time using his new Pester Balls. The Professor had promised they'd help him discover new types of Pokémon in the places he'd already visited.

Todd was really curious about what Pester Balls could do, so he tried them out as soon as he landed back in the River area. When he tossed Pester Balls instead of food toward the Poliwag and Bulbasaur near the beginning of the River area, they quickly showed themselves and allowed their photos to be taken. Cool!

METAPOD™
Number:11
Type: Bug

When he threw Pester Balls at the green Metapod hanging above the winding path, they dropped down lower. More great close-ups!

Now the Zero-One again approached the place where the Psyduck was swimming. Looking to his right, Todd began tossing Pester Balls into the bushes, where he suspected Pokémon were hiding. To his surprise a Porygon leaped out. Todd pressed the shutter button on his trusty camera and took pictures of this exotic-looking creature that could change colors—this one was green.

PORYGON™
Number: 137
Course: River
Photo Score: 3,540

A few moments later, when the Zero-One again floated near the strange red switch, the young photographer tossed Pester Balls at it. No luck. He tried aiming some Pester Balls at the Pokémon's beak above the switch. Suddenly, another Porygon jumped out from its hiding place. Thump! The Porygon landed directly on the switch, and it moved!

When the Porygon activates the switch, the towering metal gate opens, allowing Todd and the Zero-One to pass through.

As soon as the switch was activated, Todd heard a loud rumble. The huge metal gate he had passed earlier was now opening. It was a secret passageway!

Once the gate lifts open, Todd can see the new path.

Todd felt the river change its direction, flowing through the gate, and the Zero-One floated along. There in front of Todd was a steep waterfall, and over they went! During this free fall, Todd was thinking that the ride was getting a little too exciting! Before he could get really scared, and just before his vehicle was about to crash, its built-in air brakes kicked in. The Zero-One began to hover gently over the water. Todd was glad Professor Oak had thought of everything when he designed such a reliable and multipurpose vehicle.

The young photographer calmed down and caught his breath after the sudden drop over the waterfall, and was now safely on his way. But before he did anything else, he needed to see the Pokémon Prof and show off his latest snapshots.

After passing through the unlocked gate, whoosh! Down the steep waterfall drops the Zero-One!

"Todd, you found a split in the path! According to my research, that split should link to a new course. I've also made a link from my lab. You should go right away!" said the Professor.

Todd took the Professor's next set of directions, which showed the way to the Cave area of Pokémon Island. He began preparing for the next trek. Later, he'd return to the River area and gather a few additional shots of Pokémon he still hadn't photographed. He'd also have a chance to get better pictures of some other Pokémon to update the PKMN Report. But for now, it was off to the island's Cave area!

Pokémon Snap

Chapter 6

Todd Discovers More Pokémon in the Cave Area

Pokémon Snap

Now that Todd had both Pokémon Food and Pester Balls at his disposal, locating new types of Pokémon and photographing them would be a bit easier. The Professor's assistant was eager to begin his next expedition. Leaving the lab, the Zero-One made its way toward a new area of the island: the Cave.

"This is a scary-looking cave. I bet if I listen carefully, I'll hear lots of strange noises," thought Todd as the Zero-One plunged down another waterfall. (This time he wasn't so scared!) He and his trusty vehicle came to a rest deep within a dark underground cave. At first, everything was pitch-black. The young photographer couldn't see anything around him.

ZUBAT™
Number: 41
Type: Poison/Flying

Todd listened hard in the dark. Off in the distance, he could hear the flapping of wings. The sound grew louder, and that meant whatever was making the noise was coming closer. All of a sudden, as he stared into the creepy gloom that surrounded him, several batlike Zubat went flying by. There was no doubt about it—finding Pokémon to photograph in the darkness of the Cave was going to be a challenge.

GRIMER™
Number: 88
Course: Cave
Photo Score: 3,500

The Zero-One was now floating gently through the Cave. There was no track or path for the vehicle to follow, as before. In the dim light, Todd could just barely see some blobs on two nearby ledges—they were Grimer with large eyes, hanging around minding their own business. Todd took their pictures. More Zubat were flying about. Way up ahead was a bright light, and the Zero-One was moving toward it. The cave lightened up just a little.

Looking cautiously below his vehicle, Todd spied another Poison-type Grimer waving its lumpy arms. He tossed three Pester Balls at this creature. It instantly evolved into a Muk. Click! Click! The young photographer's camera captured an important photo of this Pokémon evolution.

Looking cautiously below his vehicle, Todd spied another Poison-type Grimer waving its lumpy arms. He tossed some food at this creature. It instantly evolved into a Muk. Click! Click!

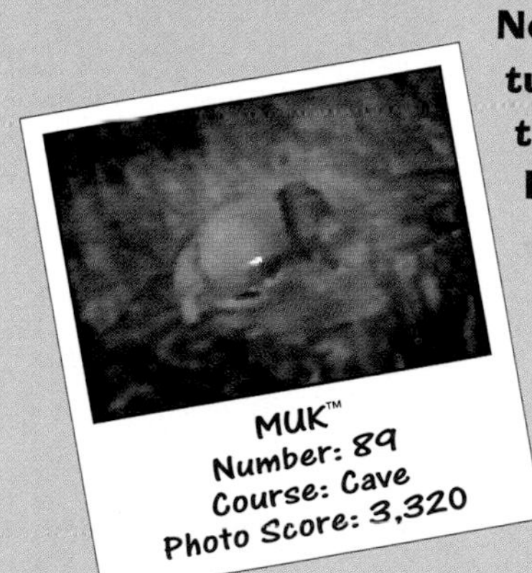

MUK™
Number: 89
Course: Cave
Photo Score: 3,320

Next, the Zero-One automatically turned to the left. Just ahead were three Bulbasaur—at least they looked like Bulbasaur right then. When Todd tossed a Pester Ball at each of these green creatures, they instantly changed into Ditto, resembling loose pink blobs of slimy goo. The Ditto had been playing a trick by disguising themselves as Bulbasaur!

Thinking back to what he had read in the Pokédex, Todd remembered that Ditto were Normal-type Pokémon that could instantly transform into other types of Pokémon. Actually seeing this happen and being able to photograph it was a special treat for the young researcher.

DITTO™
Number: 132
Course: Cave
Photo Score: 2,860

Turning his attention ahead of the Zero-One, Todd could see a little better as they got closer to the light in the distance. He spotted a Jigglypuff being

Pokémon Snap

JIGGLYPUFF™
Number: 39
Course: Cave
Photo Score: 6,350

held captive by a floating Koffing. By tossing food at the deep-purple Koffing, Todd forced this Poison-type Pokémon to let the Jigglypuff go free. Moments later, he found two more of the Pokémon, also captured and held by Koffing. Todd had to spin around several times in order to slow down his vehicle, so he could carefully aim the food he was throwing. He needed to hit all three of the disagreeable Koffing head-on. Yes! The other two Jigglypuff were soon freed, as well.

KOFFING™
Number: 109
Course: Cave
Photo Score: 3,980

Near the very bottom of the Cave was a small, crystal-clear pool of water. A yellow Weepinbell was floating around nearby, traveling in circles. Todd tossed a Pester Ball directly at this creature. Splash! It was knocked into the water. Things were quiet for about three seconds. Then suddenly a bright light started to beam out from the little pool. Todd could sense something awesome was about to happen, so he anxiously prepared his camera to take more pictures.

WEEPINBELL™
Number: 70
Course: Cave
Photo Score: 2,780

Just then, right before his eyes appeared an exotic Victreebel. It had evolved under the water! As Todd enjoyed the sight, the Victreebel posed for the camera and the eager photographer took several impressive pictures.

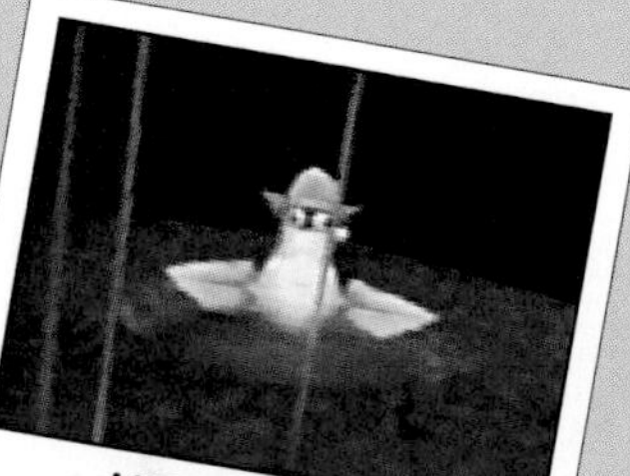

VICTREEBEL™
Number: 71
Course: Cave
Photo Score: 2,860

Looking upward, Todd saw another Zubat flying around. These batlike Pokémon were pretty common in the creepy underground Cave area, but this particular Zubat was holding onto something yellow. The Pokémon flew closer, and then the worried photographer could see the Zubat held a captive Pikachu. It was struggling to get free.

JYNX™
Number: 124
Type: Ice/Psychic

Todd immediately started throwing food and Pester Balls at the Zubat in hopes of rescuing the captive Pikachu. The problem was, the Zubat was moving around too quickly, and Todd watched it fly away with the Pikachu in tow.

Back down on the floor of the cave, the Professor's assistant found another small pool of water. In the center of this pool was another egg, colored with a beautiful pattern. There were two Jynx Pokémon asleep near the egg. Todd tried tossing food and Pester Balls at the egg, but it wouldn't budge.

JYNX™
Number: 124
Course: Cave
Photo Score: 2,780

The Zero-One started to float upward. In the distance, Todd heard singing. The sound increased as Todd's vehicle drew nearer, and then he could see the source of the beautiful music off to his right. The three Jigglypuff he had freed just minutes ago had gathered together to sing and dance. It was a wonderful scene—and it would make an incredible picture!

Just ahead was a familiar object, the Goal Gate. Todd's first journey through the Cave area was complete and had been quite successful. He couldn't wait to show Professor Oak the many unusual photos he had taken during this part of his journey.

Pokémon Snap

Todd comes across the Jigglypuff that he freed from the Koffing. He is rewarded by their happy singing and dancing.

The Goal Gate's brilliant light once again transports Todd and the Zero-One safely home to Professor Oak's lab.

Todd was awarded very high scores for many of the snapshots in his latest batch of work. But it was the photo of the three Jigglypuff that really caught Professor Oak's attention. "Wow! Isn't this Jigglypuff Trio on Stage!?!" he exclaimed. For capturing this pose on film, the young photographer earned a whopping 1,200 bonus points.

When the Professor noticed the Jigglypuff were singing, he gave Todd an extra 1,400 points, which made the overall score for this single photo worth 5,800. This was clearly the most valuable photo Todd had taken since his visit to

Pokémon Island began. "Your work is impeccable!" said his mentor proudly.

"Wow! Isn't this Jigglypuff Trio on Stage!?!" exclaimed the Professor. For capturing this pose on film, the young photographer earned a whopping 1,200 bonus points.

After the Professor evaluated his researcher's latest batch of photos, Todd received the directions to what they believed was the final unexplored area of Pokémon Island: the Valley. Before exploring this section, however, Todd wanted to try using his Pester Balls in parts of the island he'd already visited. He hoped to capture several additional types of Pokémon on film that he'd missed during earlier trips.

The tireless young photographer set a course back to the Beach area, then sat back to enjoy the ride. His trusty Zero-One eventually took him back to where he'd previously seen a large Pokémon sleeping below two flying Butterfree.

Todd needed to figure out a way to get this lazy creature to wake up long enough for him to see what it was and take its picture. After giving it some thought, he tried tossing a few Pester Balls at the Pokémon's tummy. The strategy worked! It was a Snorlax, and when it felt the light thuds of the Pester Balls on its stomach, it began to stir. Ready and waiting was Todd and his camera. Click! Click!

SNORLAX™
Number: 143
Course: Beach
Photo Score: 3,380

SCYTHER™
Number: 123
Course: Beach
Photo Score: 3,060

The Zero-One continued traveling along the sunny beach. On the left side of the track, the group of bushes Todd noticed on an earlier trip was still rustling in the wind. He began tossing a series of Pester Balls carefully into these green shrubs. This allowed him to catch a rare glimpse of a fierce green Scyther that was hiding among the leaves. As the insect-like Pokémon flew out, Todd clicked the shutter of his camera.

Todd's clever use of the Pester Balls to flush out the Scyther had another result that he didn't expect. Two dancing Pikachu on a stump appeared on some nearby tree trunks. These prancing Pikachu weren't around the last time Todd visited the Beach area, so of course he snapped a few pictures. A photo of Pikachu on a stump would be worth at least 1,300 bonus points!

After he scares the Scyther out of the bushes, two Pikachu congratulate Todd by dancing merrily on some nearby tree stumps.

When Todd passed the next set of bushes with rustling leaves, also on the left side of the track, he was lucky enough to capture another Scyther on film. This one, however, positioned itself in a fighting pose—a very rare photo, worth another 1,300 bonus points.

CHANSEY™
Number: 113
Course: Beach
Photo Score: 4,260

Next, the Professor's assistant eagerly returned to the spot where he'd seen an Eevee and previously unidentified Pokémon chasing each other. They were still there, running around some nearby rocks. Todd threw a Pester Ball, directed right at the mystery Pokémon to make it show itself. This pudgy pink Pokémon, which was rolling around in a ball as the Eevee chased it, turned out to be a lovable Chansey.

Throughout this latest trip through the Beach area, Todd continued putting the Pester Balls to work on various Pokémon to see if he could get higher-scoring snapshots. When this trek was complete, he returned to the lab, processed his latest photos, showed them to the Pokémon Prof, and then decided to revisit the Tunnel area.

Todd often wondered about that broken Power Plant in the Tunnel. How could he fix it? If he did manage to fix it, what would happen? For now, there wasn't anything he could do, but later, after he had the Poké Flute, an ingenius idea would pop into his head!

By tossing several pieces of food between the Pikachu and the egg, Todd would be able to lure his latest subject into position, much as he'd lured the Pikachu to the surfboard back at the Beach area.

Todd hopes he can fix the broken-down Power Plant that lies abandoned in the heart of the Tunnel.

Todd uses food to lure a nearby Pikachu close to the mysterious and colorful egg-shaped object.

To slow his vehicle down, Professor Oak's researcher would then spin around several times very quickly. While he was doing this, Todd would play the Poké Flute, causing the Pikachu to release a Thunder Wave attack on the egg. By tapping the Pikachu's electricity, Todd would be able to jump-start the Power Plant using Pika Power!

Moments after the Pikachu's jolt of electricity made contact with the egg, it would hatch. A giant Zapdos would pop out of the egg and the entire Tunnel would come to life with radiant light. Electricity flowing freely, the Power Plant would be fixed!

But all this would happen a little later on. For now, Todd moved past the metal doors. He wanted to snap pictures of the Diglett who was playing with the Pikachu. When the Diglett popped its head up from the ground the first time, Todd took a picture. Then he followed the Pikachu forward to where the Diglett popped its head up again. Still following the Pikachu, Todd saw one more Diglett appear. Click! Click! Moments later, Todd expected the Diglett to appear again, but not this time—instead he was amazed to see a multi-headed Dugtrio!

ZAPDOS™
Number: 145
Course: Tunnel
Photo Score: 4,320

The happy photographer snapped a few pictures of the Dugtrio, and was even more thrilled when several more Dugtrio appeared. The Zero-One was almost totally surrounded by all the heads of these Dugtrio Pokémon—an incredible photo opportunity! With power now restored to the Tunnel, there were some truly awesome sights to see.

DUGTRIO™
Number: 51
Course: Tunnel
Photo Score: 4,470

In the newly lit Tunnel, Todd can photograph all these Dugtrio.

MAGNEMITE™
Number: 81
Course: Tunnel
Photo Score: 2,930

At the very end of the Tunnel, Todd again spied some floating Magnemite and Magneton. Coaxed by Pokémon Food and Pester Balls, they allowed their photos to be taken.

What an exciting trip to the Tunnel this had been! Professor Oak was delighted by the new photos Todd had taken, and his young assistant knew he should get back to work. He still needed to revisit the Volcano area with Pester Balls and food, to seek out the Pokémon he'd missed on earlier trips. This seemed as good a time as any for a trek back to the Volcano area.

MAGNETON™
Number: 82
Course: Tunnel
Photo Score: 3,780

Once he'd returned to the Volcano, Todd turned to his supply of Pokémon Food for help. He discovered that by tossing food to a Vulpix standing over to the right, near the beginning of the area, he could lure it forward and attract several more Vulpix. With all of them gathered in one spot, he had created a splendid group photo opportunity.

By tossing out some food, Todd collects several Vulpix Pokémon into a group pose for an extra-points picture.

A bit later, the Zero-One drew near to where the red-and-yellow egg was blocking the path. Todd spotted a Charmander over to the left. He tossed it some food. This caused some unusual activity. From all directions, Charmander began to approach. They all looked almost identical, and each one wanted to chow down on the food Todd was throwing around. As more hungry Charmander appeared, Todd gave them more food.

CHARMANDER™
Number: 4
Type: Fire

Later, Poké Flute in hand, Todd would have a great idea about the egg sitting on the pathway. Instead of throwing food or Pester Balls at it, he would let it block the Zero-One, causing the vehicle to come to a stop. Tossing out more food, he would play the Poké Flute until the Charmander suddenly lined up and started marching together!

Todd tosses food to Charmander.

Then he would need to move that egg...Todd thumped it with a Pester Ball, pushing it into the nearby lava pool. The Zero-One started moving again.

The Charmander line themselves up and start marching together.

Off in the distance, to the vehicle's right, were a series of small craters. The curious researcher tossed some Pester Balls into each of the cones, wondering what would happen. Out came furry Growlithe from the first and second craters. A bigger, meaner-looking Arcanine leapt out from the third crater. More Fire-type Pokémon! Todd excitedly took several photographs.

GROWLITHE™
Number: 58
Course: Volcano
Photo Score: 3,500

As his transport moved forward through this volcanic area, Todd eventually spotted a Charmeleon walking around the edge of a lava pit. Using several Pester Balls, he aimed directly at the Charmeleon and managed to knock it into the lava. Bathing in the hot lava was a special treat for this happy Fire-type Pokémon, and it instantly evolved into a Charizard. Click! Click! Todd snapped some excellent photographs as flames shot out from the winged creature's mouth and nose.

ARCANINE™
Number: 59
Course: Volcano
Photo Score: 4,400

With a steady hand and perfect timing, Todd throws Pester Balls into the small craters. His reward is the chance to photograph a Growlithe and an Arcanine.

It's bath time for this Fire-type Pokémon! Todd uses Pester Balls to knock the Charmeleon into a lava pit.

This trip to the Volcano area was soon at an end. The Pester Balls had come in handy for finding and photographing Pokémon that Todd hadn't seen on his earlier trips. Gathering pictures for the PKMN Report was certainly an exciting project!

Pokémon Snap

Seeing a Pokémon evolution is always a special treat for a Pokémon researcher. Todd gets to see a Charmeleon change into a Charizard.

After making a return visit to the lab to see Professor Oak, young Todd plotted his next course to the Valley area of Pokémon Island, where his safari adventure would continue.

CHARIZARD™
Number: 6
Course: Volcano
Photo Score: 3,740

Pokémon Snap

Chapter 7

Todd Surfs the Rapids through the Valley

Todd had covered a lot of territory so far on his journeys through Pokémon Island. He'd already seen and photographed over 44 different types of wild Pokémon. But young Todd's quest was far from over.

After completing his last trip to the island, he and Professor Oak had studied the Professor's map again. According to the map, the Valley was the final area of Pokémon Island. As everyone knows, however, nothing is quite what it seems in the world of Pokémon. Even though the map showed only one more place left to explore, who knew what it would reveal? The determined young photographer wasn't about to leave the island for good until the PKMN Report was totally complete.

Todd revved up the Zero-One and set a direct course to the Valley. As usual, it was a very short trip. Within moments, the Zero-One had reached its destination. SPLASH! Todd's vehicle landed smack in the middle of a very turbulent river.

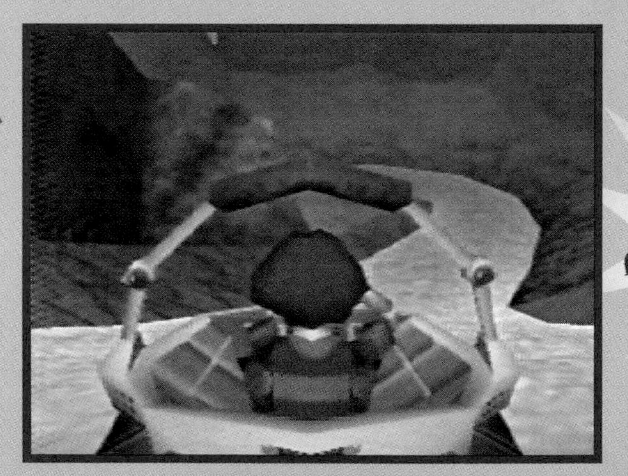

The Valley's river was flowing much faster than the one in the River area!

Looking around quickly, Todd realized this was not the same peaceful stream he had traveled in the island's River area. He and the Zero-One were at the bottom of a waterfall, about to be swept away by the swift-flowing

water. He grabbed his stash of Pokémon Food and Pester Balls and prepared for what he was sure would be an exciting and fast-paced expedition through the Valley.

SQUIRTLE™
Number: 7
Type: Water

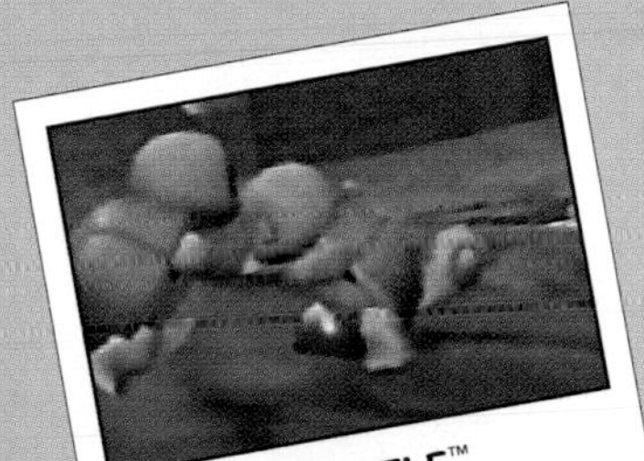

SQUIRTLE™
Number: 7
Course: Valley
Photo Score: 3,230

When the vehicle started moving forward, Todd immediately noticed three round, brown objects floating in the water just ahead of him. He tossed Pester Balls at these objects, which caused them to bounce toward the land. Only then did the young photographer realize these were Squirtle and what he'd seen floating in the river were the turtle-like shells on their backs. To get even better pictures as the Squirtle began jumping around on the riverbank, Todd threw 'em some food.

The Zero-One followed the river as it veered to the left. Over on Todd's right and way off in the distance, an odd-looking Sandshrew was hopping up and down on the land. Unfortunately, it was too far away for Todd to get a good photo at the moment, but he clicked the shutter of his camera anyway to capture the pudgy Pokémon on film.

MAGIKARP™
Number: 129
Course: Valley
Photo Score: 2,840

Here on the river Todd hoped to catch a glimpse of a Magikarp or other fishlike Pokémon, so he began throwing Pester Balls into the water ahead of him. One of the Pester Balls caused a Magikarp to jump out of the water. It landed on shore, near the Mankey, which then knocked the Magikarp over the nearby hill. The Mankey then came running toward the river, allowing Todd to snap a close-up picture of it. This all happened very quickly.

SANDSHREW™
Number: 27
Course: Valley
Photo Score: 3,880

Floating past the hill over which the Magikarp had disappeared, Todd noticed several Geodude climbing the steep cliffs of the mountainside. He was eager to snap pictures of these creatures, but they were facing the mountain, not his camera. Pester Balls would work, he thought as he threw some directly at the Geodude. This caused them to drop down to the ground and turn toward the Zero-One. Click! Click! The clever photographer was rewarded with several excellent pictures of the rock-climbing Pokémon with their round bodies and extra-long arms. Meanwhile, several more Sandshrew appeared close to the edge of the river, and allowed themselves to be photographed.

Todd tosses Pester Balls at the climbing Geodude to make them drop back down to the ground. This forces them to face Todd's camera.

In a very short time, Todd had photographed three more kinds of Pokémon for the report. Those Pester Balls were sure coming in handy! Hoping for an even better shot of the Geodude, the young photographer

GEODUDE™
Number: 74
Course: Valley
Photo Score: 3,460

GRAVELER™
Number: 75
Course: Valley
Photo Score: 4,640

used more of the Pester Balls to knock Pokémon off the mountainside. Suddenly a yellow-and-brown Sandslash and a Rock-type Graveler came into sight, just as Todd's vehicle approached the top of a small waterfall. The Graveler was standing on the riverbank, but it started climbing briskly up the nearby cliff, giving Todd only a few moments to capture the Pokémon on film. Then, over the falls went the Zero-One.

In a very short time, Todd had photographed three more kinds of Pokémon for the report. Those Pester Balls were sure coming in handy!

At the bottom of the waterfall, a lovely yellow Staryu was floating just above the water. Snapping a picture of this small but elegant star-shaped Pokémon with its face toward the camera would be tricky. The Staryu was drifting upward while at the same time spinning around in circles. Todd snapped a series of pictures, hoping one of them would turn out to be a shot that displayed the Staryu's face. This Pokémon began following the Zero-One as it spun around.

SANDSLASH™
Number: 28
Course: Valley
Photo Score: 3,760

Looking to the left, Todd noticed the Magikarp that had been thrown over the hill just a few moments before. It had landed on the ground, near the edge of the water. Knowing that Water-type Pokémon needed to be in water, Todd threw several Pester Balls at the Magikarp, helping it to fall back into the river. The revived Magikarp swam head-on into the cascading water of a nearby waterfall.

STARYU™
Number: 120
Course: Valley
Photo Score: 3,020

Seconds later, the Professor's assistant heard a loud roar coming from behind that same waterfall.

GYARADOS™
Number: 130
Course: Valley
Photo Score: 4,480

Turning his head to the right, he saw the giant head and neck of a Gyarados pop out. Todd snapped a few pictures and was relieved when his Zero-One continued down the river, putting some distance between him and the angry Gyarados.

Now two more Staryu appeared in front of the Zero-One. Todd took pictures to get them to float in the air around the vehicle, following a circular path. Click! Click!

STARMIE™
Number: 121
Course: Valley
Photo Score: 3,080

Then he looked ahead and saw, on the right and near the middle of the river, a swirling whirlpool. The Staryu were heading right for it! All three of the Staryu got sucked into the whirlpool and disappeared. Instantly, they evolved into Starmie and managed to escape from the rapidly-spinning water. Todd was so fascinated that he barely remembered to snap pictures as the newly evolved, star-shaped Pokémon floated away in the air.

Before Todd could think what to do, all three of the Staryu got sucked into the whirlpool and disappeared.

Next to the whirlpool, a small Dratini leapt out of the water and then quickly dove back in. As the Professor's assistant watched, the eel-like Pokémon appeared and then disappeared several times.

Each time Todd takes photos of the Staryu, it begins floating in circles around the Zero-One.

Todd had already figured out that there was definitely something special about the whirlpool. Turning his head to face it as the Zero-One floated past, the curious photographer tossed several Pester Balls into its center. He was excited and very surprised when a big winged Dragonite came flying up out of the water and hovered playfully in the air. Click! Click! The eager young photographer's camera caught this Pokémon on film.

DRATINI™
Number: 147
Course: Valley
Photo Score: 2,960

While the Zero-One floated rapidly down-river, Todd occasionally tossed Pester Balls into the water, hoping to catch additional glimpses of other Dratini, or maybe even a Goldeen or Magikarp. The Pester Balls did their job well, and caused several Water-type Pokémon to make appearances.

DRAGONITE™
Number: 149
Course: Valley
Photo Score: 4,320

Todd grabs his camera and snaps a photo of the Dragonite as it emerges from the whirlpool.

Directly ahead, but quite a ways in the distance, Todd could see the Goal Gate. In front of it, he noticed the metallic gleam of another gate. It looked very much like the metal gate he'd seen near the end of the River. This one was also locked. Was there another area of the island he hadn't yet explored, beyond the gate? He needed to find a way to unfasten that huge door.

GOLDEEN™
Number: 118
Course: Valley
Photo Score: 3,220

On the ground just before the gate, to the right of the Zero-One, there was a large red switch. Too bad—Todd hadn't noticed this switch until after the Zero-One drifted past it. For now, he wouldn't have a chance to figure out how to activate it. Instead, the Professor's apprentice decided to relax for a few moments as his vehicle was automatically guided through the Goal Gate.

Todd had 52 snapshots from this trip, and he needed to sort through all of them and choose which ones he'd show the Professor. By now, he had a pretty good idea of what Professor Oak was looking for and what types of photos would earn the most points.

Todd notices another metal gate and wonders what it leads to. He also spots the red switch on the bank as the Zero-One heads for the Goal Gate.

Todd had successfully captured the two Squirtle playing together in one picture!

Todd had successfully captured the two Squirtle playing together in one picture! Even better, the Pokémon were centered in the frame. His teacher really liked this shot and awarded Todd 3,230 points for it. "Wonderful!" said the Professor as he admired the young photographer's latest work. He awarded an additional 3,800 points for the snapshot of the Graveler.

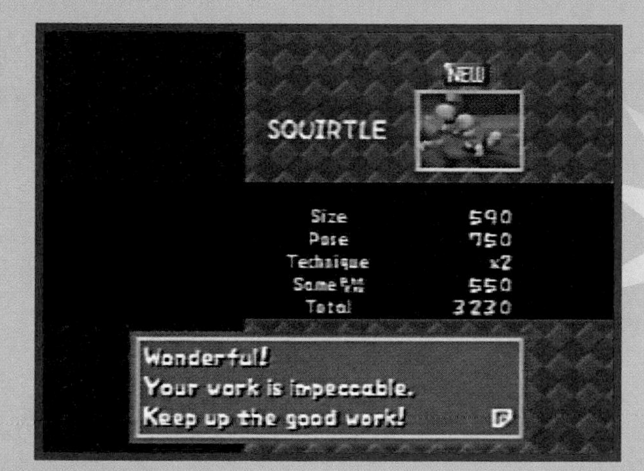

Professor Oak likes what he sees when Todd displays the shot of the two frisky Squirtle.

GRAVELER™
Number: 75
Type: Rock/Ground

By the time the Pokémon Prof finished looking at Todd's snapshots taken during his first trip to the Valley, photos of 52 kinds of Pokémon had been added to the PKMN Report, and Todd had earned a total of 150,650 points. He was really making excellent progress. It was now time for the young photographer to take another pass through the Valley. This time through, Todd intended to find a way to activate the red switch, certain that it would open the metal gate.

MANKEY™
Number: 56
Course: Valley
Photo Score: 3,560

A few moments after passing the whirlpool once again, the photographer caught sight of three Squirtle at the foot of a hill. At the very top of the hill, a fierce Fighting-type Mankey was waving its arms. Two Squirtle suddenly ran up the hill, and the third stayed at the bottom and hid in its shell.

Patiently, Todd waited until the Zero-One was directly next to the third Squirtle. The photographer was now watching the riverbank on his right as the river carried his vehicle forward. He tossed a Pester Ball directly at the Squirtle. Yes! A direct hit on the Squirtle made it shoot up the hill and hit the Mankey head-on. This sent the Mankey tumbling down the other side of the mountain.

As the Zero-One drifted around a bend in the river, Todd spotted the same Mankey. It was standing near the red switch! Todd acted quickly, tossing some Pester Balls at the Mankey, causing it to fly back and land on the switch. The gate began to open! Sure enough, just as Todd had thought might happen, the flow of the river changed direction. Through the gate floated the Zero-One with its very happy passenger.

As he gets lined up with the Squirtle and the Mankey, Todd tosses a Pester Ball at the Squirtle.

Todd found himself in a totally new area of the Valley. Whad'ya know! Standing on the nearby shore was Professor Oak. "Oh! Hi, Todd! What a surprise to see you here! I suppose you'd like to know why I am here? Ahh, well, I received some interesting information at the Pokémon Lab. It seems that there are six PKMN Signs hidden on this island. They have something to do with important Pokémon that are here. The Signs are scenery which seem to resemble Pokémon," said the Professor.

The curious young researcher paid careful attention to everything his friend was saying. "One Sign is a mountain that looks like Dugtrio. I am here to look for it. However, I can't go any deeper into the island, so I can't find it. Have you seen a mountain that looks like Dugtrio? Oh! I have an idea! If you find this PKMN Sign, take a picture of it like you would a Pokémon. We might discover clues from the pictures and the places you took them," added the Pokémon Prof.

DUGTRIO™
Number: 51
Type: Ground

Todd readily agreed to begin searching for the various PKMN Signs. As he was about to depart, the

Professor said, "Wait...I will add a page for PKMN Signs in the PKMN Report." Now, in addition to finding and photographing the wild Pokémon living on the island, Todd needed to locate and take pictures of the six PKMN Signs.

Professor Oak surprises Todd in the heart of the Valley, telling him about the PKMN Signs hidden throughout the island.

To make the job a bit easier, Professor Oak gave his assistant another present. "Wouldn't it be great if the Zero-One moved faster?" asked the Professor. "Well, now you can use this Dash Engine if you want to go faster." The Dash Engine add-on for the Zero-One was very easy to use. Todd could activate the Dash Engine anytime he wanted his vehicle to travel at faster speeds. He thanked his mentor for this important gift.

"Wouldn't it be great if the Zero-One moved faster?" asked the Professor. "Well, now you can use this Dash Engine if you want to go faster."

Before Todd returned to his expedition, the Professor suggested he check out the PKMN Report. There it was—the added page for the PKMN Signs. It was time for the next trek back to the Valley, to find the first PKMN Sign.

Chapter 8

The Search for the Signs

Todd began thinking about his newest assignment to locate and photograph the six PKMN Signs. He wondered what these Signs actually meant and tried to decide how he'd recognize each one when he saw it. After all, he had already traveled through each area of Pokémon Island, but he didn't remember any natural scenery that had looked like Pokémon. But then again, he hadn't exactly been looking for this type of thing, either.

In the PKMN Report, he studied the new section added by Professor Oak, hoping to get some clues about the Signs. There were six colored squares, each representing one of the PKMN Signs. Hmmm...

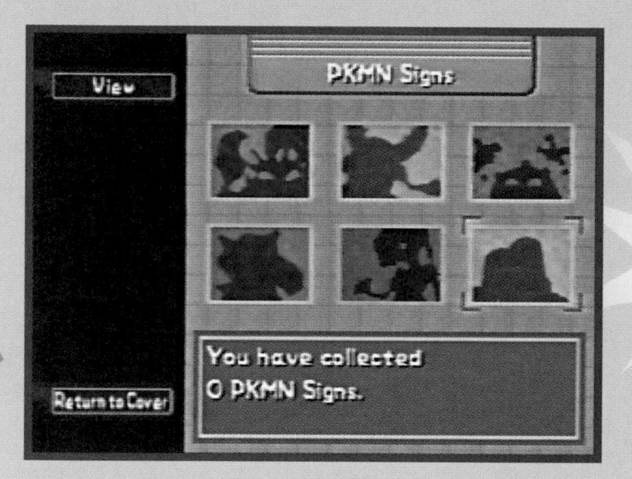

Todd checks out the new Sign section of the PKMN Report.

When Todd returned to the Valley, his goal was to uncover the first PKMN Sign, and of course, try to take some higher-scoring pictures of Pokémon he'd already found and photographed. His trusty Zero-One was now equipped with the Dash Engine, and there was still plenty of Pokémon Food and Pester Balls on hand. Everything was ready.

Once again, Todd's transport landed with a splash at the bottom of a waterfall. Very soon after the start of his journey, the Zero-One followed a bend in the river to the right, and Todd saw something interesting. It was a mountain formation that looked exactly like a Dugtrio! This was it—the PKMN Sign he was searching for! The young photographer grabbed his camera and eagerly started shooting pictures of this first Sign.

Todd is excited when he spots the first PKMN Sign—a mountain formation shaped just like a Dugtrio. Click! Click!

After capturing the Dugtrio Sign on film, the remainder of Todd's journey through the Valley was uneventful. Along the way he managed to get some excellent close-up pictures of several Pokémon.

Returning to the lab, Todd developed his latest photographic creations. When the Professor took a look at the pictures of the PKMN Sign, he said, "Is this Diglett? No, it's Dugtrio! I will call this Mt. Dugtrio!" Because Todd had earned 130,000 points, he received the Poké Flute!

When the Professor took a look at the pictures of the PKMN Sign, he said, "Is this Diglett? No, it's Dugtrio! I will call this Mt. Dugtrio!"

"To make your work easier, here is a present for you," said the Professor. "Would you like to see rare Pokémon poses? Play the Pokémon Flute to make it happen! It's easy to use!"

The Pokémon Flute could play three different melodies. Professor Oak suggested to his researcher that he play this instrument often while traveling throughout the island. This was an awesome gift! Like the Pokémon Food and Pester Balls, the flute would give Todd lots of help getting Pokémon to pose for even better pictures.

There were still five more PKMN Signs to locate, and the Professor's apprentice decided to continue his search back at the Beach. To see how the flute would affect the various wild Pokémon, he began playing it for all of them as his journeys progressed.

Just ahead was the Pikachu playing near the surfboard. Todd whipped out the flute and played a happy tune. The little yellow creature started to yell, "Pi-ka-chu!" as it leaped into the air—and then it launched a whole bunch of lightning bolts in all directions. What a wonderful sight—and what a cool picture!

The little yellow creature started to yell, "Pi-ka-chu!" as it leaped into the air—and then it launched a whole bunch of lightning bolts in all directions. What a wonderful sight—and what a cool picture!

Now the Zero-One was carrying its excited passenger near the sleeping Snorlax. Todd began playing another melody. The big-bellied creature actually woke up and started dancing! For this lazy Pokémon, that was a major accomplishment! Click! Click! This was a picture Todd thought the Pokémon Prof would really like to see.

When it hears the Pokémon Flute, the Pikachu near the surfboard jumps up and releases a dazzling display of lightning bolts.

Todd still needed to find the hidden PKMN Sign located somewhere in this area. Just ahead was the Goal Gate, yet he still hadn't yet spotted the Sign. He returned to the lab and plotted a course to the Beach. Gazing down the lovely beach to the left, near where his island safari had first begun, he spotted a formation of bushes and rocks that he thought looked a little like a Kingler. He snapped several pictures.

Playing the Poké Flute awakens the sleeping Snorlax.

"This is exactly the PKMN Sign I've been looking for!" exclaimed the Professor when Todd returned to the lab. "Wonderful! If you collect all of the PKMN Signs, you will be able to enter a secret course. Isn't it amazing that a simple rock like this turned out to be a PKMN Sign? If you look at it from this angle, it looks like a Kingler. I will call this Kingler Rock!" Todd knew that a Kingler was a Water-type Pokémon, but he hadn't seen any living on the island.

On the Beach, Todd takes pictures of what turns out to be Kingler Rock–the second PKMN Sign he'd found.

Todd's search for the third PKMN Sign soon began in the Tunnel. Again, the Professor's apprentice used the Poké Flute to get the attention of the different types of Pokémon, hoping to get them to pose for close-up photos. Returning to the room with the Power Plant, Todd convinced the nearby Pikachu to release some of its electricity. Doing this caused the Zapdos to hatch from the nearby egg. The newly hatched Zapdos then gave the Power Plant another dose of their powerful electricity.

ZAPDOS™
Number: 145
Type: Electric/Flying

On the side of a nearby building, the projector was creating a shadow. Todd stared at it and realized the moving shadow looked just like the Bug-type Pokémon called a Pinsir.

The Zero-One carried Todd into the next room. Looking to the right, he saw two huge movie screens. They were showing pictures of Pokémon! There was the movie projector, now all powered up and fully operational. On the side of a nearby building, the projector was creating a shadow. Todd stared at it and realized the moving shadow looked just like the Bug-type Pokémon called a Pinsir. He figured this was another PKMN Sign as he pressed the shutter button on his camera.

When Professor Oak saw this snapshot of the Pinsir-shaped shadow, he declared, "It was very clever of you to activate the generator with Zapdos's electric shock. This shadow looks like Pinsir. I will call this Pinsir Shadow!"

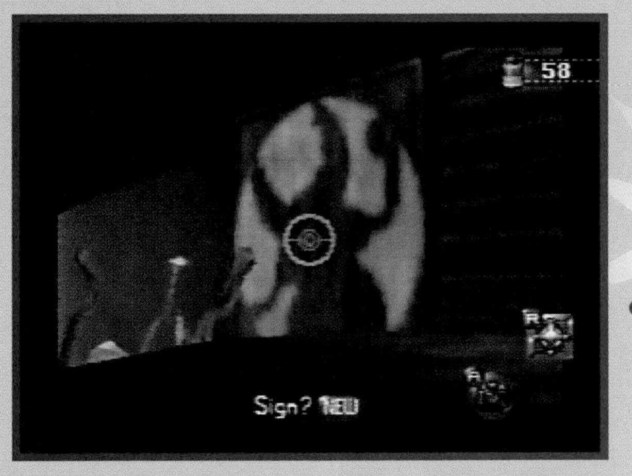

Todd sees another PKMN Sign in the shadow of the projector, which is running on electricity from the revived Power Plant.

Although spotting Mt. Dugtrio in the Valley had been pretty easy, finding the other PKMN Signs was proving to be a challenge. Todd expected to find the fourth Sign in the Volcano area, which is where he travelled next.

Right at the start of this super-hot place, just after a Rapidash Pokémon galloped directly in front of the Zero-One, Todd saw a small volcano to the left and tossed Pester Balls directly into it. Smoke started rising up...but this was no ordinary smoke. As the young photographer watched, the smoke rose into the sky and gradually took on the shape of a Poison-type Koffing. The fourth PKMN Sign was really a dark, gray cloud of smoke! Todd grabbed his camera and took a picture.

KOFFING™
Number: 109
Type: Poison

Later, the Professor exclaimed, "You hit it with a Pester Ball? Ha, ha, ha! This Smoke looks like Koffing. I will call this Koffing Smoke!"

In the Volcano area, the fourth PKMN Sign is smokin'!

CLOYSTER™
Number: 91
Course: River
Photo Score: 3,540

It was in the River area that the young photographer would ultimately find the fifth PKMN Sign. Todd set off on another journey through this area, paying careful attention to his surroundings, hoping to spot something out of the ordinary.

The Zero-One drew near the swimming Psyduck, just before the spot where Speed Pikachu was playing. Several Cloyster were leaping out of the water. It took perfect timing for Todd to capture one of these exotic Water-type Pokémon on film as they bounced up and down from the water into the air.

Floating along the river, Todd remembered the large, mushroom-shaped Pokémon that was hiding underground on the right, across from the first pink Slowpoke. Maybe the flute would draw this mystery Pokémon out into view. Todd started playing a cheerful tune, and out popped the Pokémon. It was a Vileplume! When it heard the music, the funny-looking creature started dancing and flipping around. What an amusing sight! Click! Click! Todd's camera caught the dancing Vileplume on film.

VILEPLUME™
Number: 45
Course: River
Photo Score: 2,840

Todd looked upward, above the Vileplume. Hmmm...did that tree look a little like a Ground-type Cubone? Click! Click! Yep, this was definitely another PKMN Sign!

Later, when Todd presented his photo of the PKMN Sign, Professor Oak said, "The tree looked dim because of Vileplume's powder. Hmm...It looks like Cubone. I will call this the Cubone Tree!"

The tree rising high above the nearby Vileplume looks a little like a Cubone–the fifth PKMN Sign!

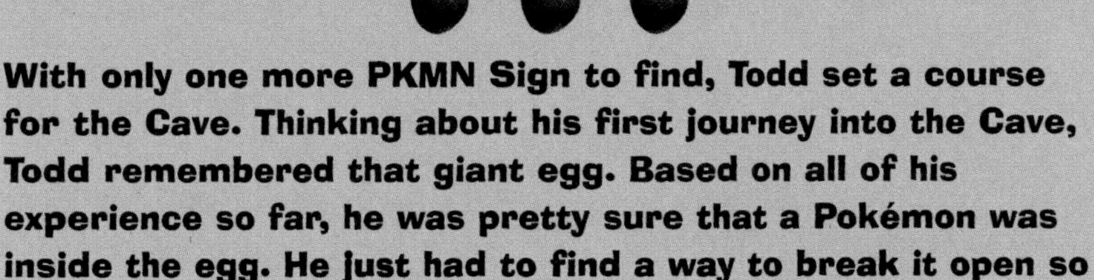

With only one more PKMN Sign to find, Todd set a course for the Cave. Thinking about his first journey into the Cave, Todd remembered that giant egg. Based on all of his experience so far, he was pretty sure that a Pokémon was inside the egg. He just had to find a way to break it open so the Pokémon could get out.

Meanwhile, there was that flying Zubat again, with a Pikachu still held tight in its claws. This time, young Todd was persistent. He kept tossing food and Pester Balls at the Zubat until it dropped its helpless prisoner. The Pikachu started to fall toward the ground! All of a sudden, a bunch of colorful balloons magically appeared on the Pikachu's back, and the lovable yellow creature began to float gently down. Click! Click! Todd took an incredible photo of Balloon Pikachu, who kept yelling "Pika! Pika!" as he landed softly near the egg on the floor of the Cave.

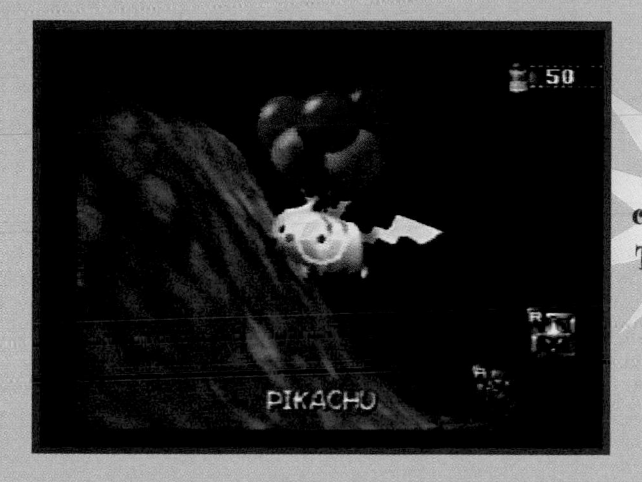

By freeing the Pikachu from the claws of the Zubat, Todd gets a photograph of Balloon Pikachu.

The Zero-One carried Todd closer to the egg and the freed Pikachu. The two Jynx were still sleeping nearby, too. Todd played the Poké Flute and the Pikachu released one of its mighty Thunder Wave attacks, causing powerful lightning bolts to hit the egg. At the very same moment, Todd tossed food at the egg.

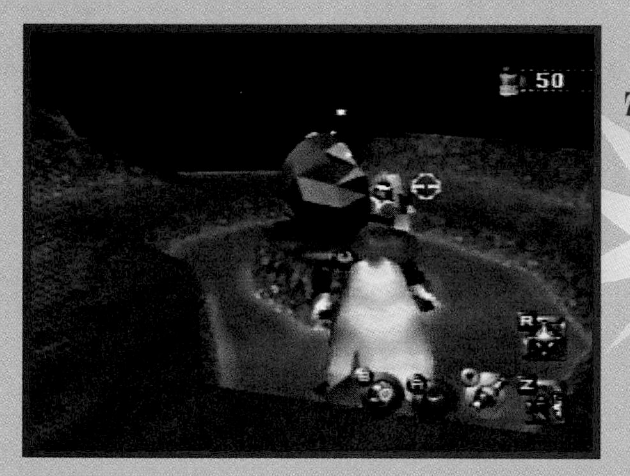

Zap! The Pikachu's Thunder Wave shoots powerful lightning bolts at the egg. Meanwhile, Todd tosses food at it.

Then, all at once, light blazed out and the Jynx creatures woke up and started waving their arms at the egg. It hatched! Out came a graceful blue Articuno. It offered the Pikachu a ride on its back, and off they soared.

The Pikachu hops onto the back of the newly hatched Articuno, and they glide majestically away.

By discovering how to release the Articuno from its egg and then taking its picture, Todd had now gathered photographs of every type of Pokémon living in the Cave area.

ARTICUNO™
Number: 144
Course: Cave
Photo Score: 4,300

As he continued his search for the sixth and final Sign, the young photographer began to wonder what would be revealed. He had carefully studied the Professor's map, and there was no area of Pokémon Island that he hadn't visited...at least that's what Todd thought.

This last Sign turned out to be the trickiest one yet to uncover. Partway through the Cave area, Todd noticed a series of sparkling stones. They looked sort of like a formation of stars, but to his eyes, they didn't really look like a Pokémon. The curious photographer snapped a few pictures of these glimmering objects anyway and brought them to the Professor.

When he developed his latest pictures, Todd noticed that the scattering of stones did, in fact, look like a constellation of stars. Then Professor Oak took a look. "I had no idea what this was about until I saw your picture," said the Professor. "I think this looks like Mewtwo! Could this be the constellation called Mewtwo? You finally got all of the PKMN Sign pictures! Hmm...After looking at these six pictures, I've noticed that the Signs are just like the constellations that can be seen from Pokémon Island! That's the key to this mystery! Now it all makes sense! It's the sky!"

"I think this looks like Mewtwo! Could this be the constellation called Mewtwo? You finally got all of the PKMN Sign pictures!"

Professor Oak added, "Rainbow Cloud, floating in the sky, is the secret course! Someone in the clouds must have created the PKMN Signs! I have made a new path to Rainbow Cloud. This could prove very important for Pokémon research. Good luck, Todd!"

When Professor Oak identifies Todd's latest picture as a constellation of stars called Mewtwo, it's the final clue to unravel the mystery of the PKMN Signs.

Now things started making sense to Todd as well. Rainbow Cloud was a secret area located in the sky, high above the island. Visiting this mysterious place was going to be very exciting. Each of the PKMN Signs represented one of the star formations Todd could see when he looked directly upward into the sky at night. These clues led him and the Professor to figure out that the secret area was not located on Pokémon Island—it could be found high above it.

The Professor had to program the Zero-One to find the Rainbow Cloud. When that was done, Todd jumped into his vehicle and got ready to see what new surprises were awaiting him.

Pokémon Snap

Chapter 9

To Rainbow Cloud and Beyond!

Boosted by the Dash Engine, the Zero-One took off like a rocket! Instead of crossing land and water, traveling to remote destinations around Pokémon Island, Todd and his vehicle zoomed upward into the sky. High above the island, somewhere near that faraway place where the planet's atmosphere meets outer space, was where Rainbow Cloud was located.

Here in this magical realm, Todd would be able to observe and photograph the rarest-of-rare species of Pokémon—a Mew. All of his cleverness and his photo-taking skills would be put to the test, because the bright white, exotic Mew would not be easy to capture on film.

When Todd arrived on Rainbow Cloud, there wasn't too much to see at first. The Zero-One was floating on a giant cloud. Looking in every direction, all Todd could see were dazzling stars and the vastness of empty space.

Looking in every direction, all Todd could see were dazzling stars and the vastness of empty space.

But wait—what was that? From off to the right, Todd heard a purring sound. "M-e-e-w!" Suddenly, there it was! It was trapped within some sort of a clear bubble floating in space! Amazed, Todd could barely control his excitement as he eagerly lifted his camera. But when Todd tried to focus the camera on the catlike Mew, he couldn't take the picture. The bubble surrounding the Mew was some sort of barrier, and the photo couldn't be snapped.

The clever young photographer immediately began tossing food at the bubble. After each direct hit, he could hear a crashing sound, and the bubble with the Mew inside went flying off into space.

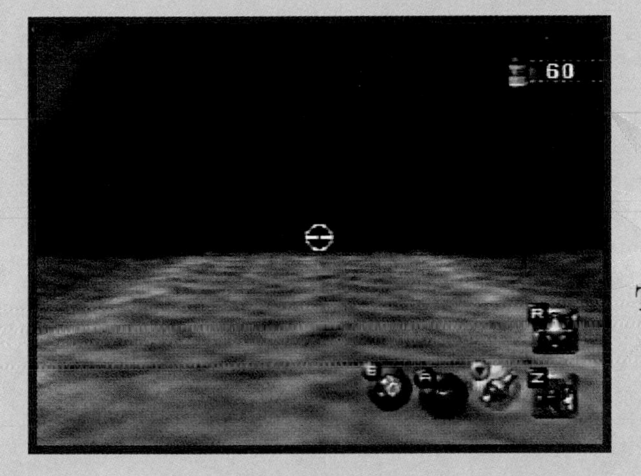

As the Zero-One reaches its destination on Rainbow Cloud, Todd can see stars everywhere.

Within seconds, however, it came floating back. Todd kept throwing food at the bubble as it drifted randomly in various directions.

Finally, after three direct hits, the bubble turned yellow, but the Mew was still trapped inside. Not willing to give up, Todd kept tossing food at the strange bubble each time it floated near the Zero-One. He was determined to set the Mew free.

For the first time ever, Todd sees a Mew up close. But the bubble keeps him from taking an all-important photograph.

It was a good thing Todd had had so much practice—he needed perfect aim in order to keep thumping the bubble

with the food. At last, after several more direct hits, the Mew managed to escape! Todd grabbed his camera and started snapping pictures. Click! Click! Unfortunately, within seconds, the bubble reappeared and again imprisoned the Mew.

At last, after several more direct hits, the Mew finally managed to escape! Todd grabbed his camera and started snapping pictures.

Once more, Todd began throwing food at the bubble, hoping to release this extraordinary Pokémon and take additional pictures to show the Professor. When the Mew finally got loose again, the young photographer tossed more food, this time directly at the lovely white creature. This caused it to spin around and around in circles. But the Mew didn't float away from Todd and the Zero-One. The next time it was hit with food, it stayed where it was. Perfect! Again and again the delighted photographer pressed the shutter button, getting some truly incredible close-ups.

By freeing the rare and awesome Mew from the bubble, Todd can take the most important pictures of the entire expedition. What an opportunity!

Todd's journey to Rainbow Cloud ended without warning as he passed suddenly through the Goal Gate.

Todd's chance to photograph the rare Mew soon came to an end. From out of nowhere, a Goal Gate appeared and transported the young photographer directly back to the lab.

Todd was so thrilled! He had actually seen a Mew, and he could barely stand still and wait for his new photos to be developed. Out of all the snapshots he'd taken, Todd chose his favorite and brought it directly to the Pokémon Prof.

Of course, when the Professor saw Todd's picture of the Mew, he immediately awarded bonus points for it. In fact, Todd received a whole bundle of extra points from this trip to Rainbow Cloud. For starters, because this was The Rare Pokémon Mew, Todd received 2,500 points for the photo. Since the Pokémon took up most of the frame, he earned 890 more points. The pose of the Mew in the photo was so spectacular, Professor Oak added another 1,500 points to the overall score. Todd's photographic technique was also excellent. The Mew was right in the center of the frame. For this, the Professor doubled Todd's score.

MEW™
Number: 151
Course: Rainbow
Photo Score: 9,870

Pokémon Snap

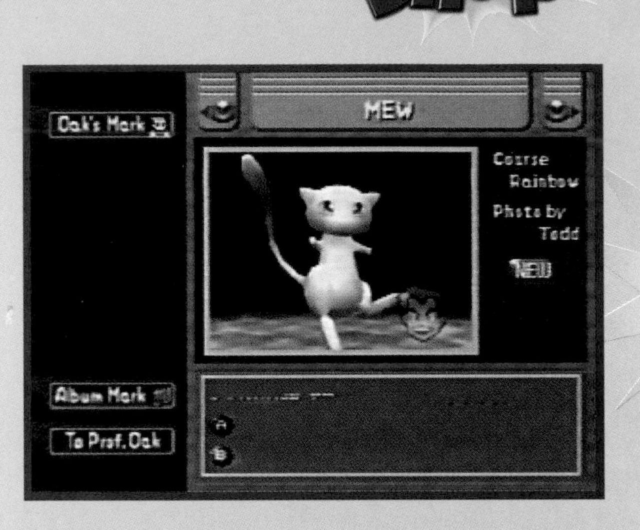

Which photo to choose? Finally, Todd decides on the perfect shot to show Professor Oak.

"Wonderful! Your work is impeccable," exclaimed the Professor as he totaled up the amazing score Todd earned for this single photo. Out of a maximum 10,000 points, the photographer received 9,780! This was his best effort of all!

Out of a maximum 10,000 points, the photographer received 9,780! This was his best effort of all!

Professor Oak awards a whopping 9,780 points for Todd's picture of the Mew!

"You made it, Todd! I never believed that Mew lived on this island! Our PKMN Report now has a very memorable picture. Thank you, Todd. This is all because of your hard work. It was so nice to find a photographer as good as you," said the Professor proudly.

The PKMN Report was just about complete! Todd had managed to photograph all 63 different types of Pokémon living on the island. Instead of calling it quits, however, Todd and the Pokémon Prof decided to work a bit more on this important research.

The PKMN Report was just about complete! Todd had managed to photograph all 63 different types of Pokémon living on the island.

Reviewing the Report and sorting the entries by point score, Todd was able to see which of his photos earned the highest and lowest scores. To make the report even better, the Professor's assistant decided he should return to various areas of the island and try to improve the Pokémon pictures that had earned him the lowest point scores. Now that Todd knew his way around Pokémon Island and understood all of its secrets, getting through each environment and reshooting the pictures he needed wouldn't be too difficult.

Finally, after making several more treks through the island's sections, both Todd and Professor Oak were extremely pleased with how the PKMN Report turned out.

During the time these two Pokémon researchers worked together, they learned a great deal about wild Pokémon and their everyday lives in their natural habitats. This was very meaningful research that until now, nobody else had ever done. Their research would help Pokémon fans and trainers everywhere to better understand these lovable creatures.

Todd was sad, however, when his work at last came to an end. The Professor assured his assistant that they'd soon be able to work together again on another project. This made Todd very happy. Like everyone else living in the World of Pokémon, Todd had tremendous respect for the Pokémon Prof, and he also loved learning about the wild Pokémon.

In fact, young Todd was well on his way to becoming a well-known and highly successful Pokémon researcher in his own right. This made his teacher very proud. Todd even had the chance to make copies of his favorite Pokémon pix and create his own personal album. It would be a very special souvenir to help him remember the most exciting moments of his expedition.

What a wonderful experience it had been!

Photo Score Index